THE COMPLETE AIR FRYER COOKBOOK FOR BEGINNERS

Discover lots of healthy and delicious recipes to prepare quickly, using British ingredients and European measurements

Olivia J. Ward

INTRODUCTION

As a modern resident of the United Kingdom, you have likely come to appreciate the sheer variety and cultural influences that define our diverse cuisine. From traditional British classics to fusion dishes inspired by far-off lands, our collective palate has expanded considerably throughout the years. The aim of this cookbook is to incorporate that same delightful diversity into your air-frying forays while staying true to our roots in the UK.

The beauty of an air fryer lies in its ability to deliver that much-adored crispy texture without relying heavily on calorie-laden oils and fats -- allowing you to savour healthier and guilt-free meals without sacrificing flavour or satisfaction. Lending itself perfectly to busy lifestyles, this ingenious appliance promises minimal mess, reduced cooking time and unparalleled ease of use.

Navigating through these recipes, you'll encounter familiar favourites reimagined for the modern air fryer alongside exciting new offerings that will undoubtedly inspire your inner experimental chef. From crispy fish and chips to vegetable wedges infused with fresh herbs, this cookbook ensures something for everyone.

Accompanied by detailed instructions and vivid imagery, even those new to air frying will find themselves scaling their way up the culinary ladder in no time. So, we invite you, dear reader, to roll up your sleeves, switch on your air fryer, and prepare to immerse yourself in the splendid realm of captivating UK flavours while learning to harness the power of air frying technology. Happy cooking and bon appétit!

BENEFITS OF AIR FRYING COMPARED TO TRADITIONAL FRYING

One such revolutionary approach to enjoying our favourite fried foods without the guilt is air frying. In this chapter, we will explore the benefits of air frying compared to traditional frying methods and how it can positively impact our overall well-being while still satisfying our cravings for crispy, delectable dishes.

1. Healthier Results- One of the primary benefits of air frying is that it uses considerably less oil compared to traditional frying methods. Traditional frying involves submerging food in a large amount of hot oil, which can cause the food to absorb a significant quantity of fat and calories. On the other hand, air frying requires little or no oil, relying on heated air to cook and brown the food instead. As a result, air-fried meals contain fewer calories and less fat than their traditionally fried counterparts.

2. Less Mess- Anyone who has cooked using traditional frying methods knows it can be a messy endeavour. Splattering oil and greasy countertops are common occurrences when you fry food in a pan or deep fryer. Air frying eliminates these challenges as the cooking process is contained within the air fryer itself. Additionally, many models come with dishwasher-safe parts, making clean-up even more effortless.

3. Reduces the Risk Of Acrylamide Formation- Acrylamide is a potentially harmful substance that can form when certain foods are cooked at high temperatures through processes like frying or baking. According to research, consuming acrylamide may increase the risk of developing cancer. Air frying has been shown to reduce acrylamide formation by up to 90% compared to traditional deep-frying methods, making it a safer choice when preparing your favourite fried dishes.

4. Versatility- Air fryers are incredibly versatile appliances that can do much more than just fry foods without excess oil. They can also be used for roasting, baking, and grilling, making them a valuable addition to any kitchen. With an air fryer, you can experiment with a wide range of recipes, from crispy French fries to juicy grilled chicken.

5. Time and Energy Efficiency- Air frying can be more time-efficient compared to traditional frying methods. Since air fryers heat up faster than an oven or deep fryer, they can reduce overall cooking times. They are also more energy-efficient as they do not require a large amount of electricity to maintain their high temperatures.

From healthier results with less oil, reduced mess during cooking, decreased acrylamide formation, increased versatility, and improved time and energy efficiency - it is easy to see why so many people are adopting this modern cooking method. If you haven't already, consider trying an air fryer for your next delicious and guilt-free fried meal.

HOW AN AIR FRYER WORKS

An air fryer is a modern kitchen appliance that has revolutionized healthy cooking by enabling people to enjoy their favourite fried foods with little or no oil. This innovative gadget uses hot air circulation technology to cook food, giving it a crispy exterior and tender interior while significantly reducing the calorie and fat content compared to traditional deep-frying methods.

The air fryer is designed with a compact countertop appliance, usually having a removable basket or tray where the food is placed during the cooking process. The key component of an air fryer is its heating element, which generates high temperatures needed for cooking. In addition, it features a powerful fan that helps circulate hot air around the food at high speed, thereby creating a convection effect. Consequently, this hot air cooks the food evenly from all sides while retaining its moisture and avoiding excessive oil absorption.

Operating an air fryer is quite simple and user-friendly. First, you need to preheat the appliance to ensure the desired temperature is reached. Then, place the food in the basket or tray and set the timer according to the recommended cooking duration. Some advanced models are equipped with digital controls and pre-set modes for various kinds of foods like French fries, chicken wings, or vegetables, making it convenient for users.

Air fryers are highly versatile appliances that can be used for more than frying. They are also suitable for baking, roasting, and even grilling various dishes. This multi-functionality makes them attractive additions to any kitchen set up, especially for those who want healthier alternatives to regular frying methods.
One of the main advantages of an air fryer includes its ability to create delicious fried foods with up to 80% less fat compared to traditional frying techniques. This helps promote a healthier lifestyle without compromising on taste or texture. Additionally, air fryers usually cook faster than conventional ovens or stovetops due to their rapid heating and high-speed hot air circulation.

Furthermore, air fryers contribute to a safer cooking environment by significantly reducing the risk of potential oil splatters and burns commonly associated with traditional deep-frying. They also minimize odour build-up, making them a suitable option for small apartments or open-concept living.

By utilizing hot air circulation technology, it offers a healthier alternative to traditional frying methods and acts as a multi-purpose tool for cooking various types of dishes. With an air fryer in your kitchen arsenal, you can indulge in your favourite fried foods while maintaining a healthy lifestyle.

WHICH FOODS CAN BE COOKED IN AN AIR FRYER

Air fryers have been taking the culinary world by storm, providing a healthier alternative to traditional frying methods. But what foods can you actually prepare in an air fryer? In this chapter, we'll explore some of the best food choices for optimal air frying results.

1. Chips- One of the most popular and quintessential British foods, chips (or fries for our American cousins) come out crispy and delicious when cooked in an air fryer. You can use fresh or frozen chips, simply season them with salt and your favourite spices before placing them in the fryer basket.

2. Chicken- From chicken nuggets to grilled chicken breast and drumsticks, you can prepare a wide range of chicken dishes using an air fryer. The hot air circulation ensures that your chicken is cooked evenly and comes out with a satisfyingly crispy skin.

3. Roasted Vegetables- Not just limited to meats, roasted vegetables can also be cooked to perfection in an air fryer. Toss your favourite veggies in a light coating of oil and your preferred seasoning. You'll achieve crispy outsides while maintaining tender insides.

4. Sausages & Bacon- Air-frying both sausages and bacon will result in perfectly cooked, mouth-watering dishes with much less fat than traditional frying methods. Just place them in the air fryer and let the appliance do the hard work for you.

5. Fish- If you're a fan of fish and chips or other breaded fish dishes, fear not – your air fryer has got you covered! Coat your fish fillets with breadcrumbs or batter, and cook until golden brown and flaky inside.

6. Pastries & Desserts- Sweet treats are also fair game when it comes to air frying. Mince pies, fruit turnovers, and even doughnuts can be cooked using an air fryer with excellent results.

7. Quiche & Frittatas- Whip up a homemade quiche or frittata, place it in your air fryer, and let the machine do its thing. You'll be rewarded with a deliciously golden, perfectly cooked meal.

The above list is just the tip of the iceberg when it comes to foods you can prepare in an air fryer; feel free to experiment with your favourite dishes and enjoy the delicious results.

CLEANING AND MAINTENANCE OF THE AIR FRYER

Like any other appliance, keeping your air fryer clean and well-maintained is essential for the longevity and performance of the device. Here, we will explore various tips and tricks for proper cleaning and maintenance, ensuring your air fryer remains a trusty companion in your kitchen.

1. Regular Cleaning- To keep your air fryer working efficiently, make sure to clean it after each use. This will help prevent the build-up of food residue and grease, which could eventually cause damage or affect the taste of your food.

- First, unplug your air fryer and let it cool down completely before performing any cleaning.
- Next, remove the basket, tray and pan from the appliance. These parts can usually be cleaned using warm soapy water and a non-abrasive sponge. Some models may have dishwasher-safe components; check your user manual for guidance.
- Make sure to clean the interior of the air fryer as well. Use a damp cloth or sponge to wipe down the inside walls and heating element—be cautious not to damage the element.

2. Deep Cleaning- Over time, oil and grease can accumulate within your air fryer, leading to unpleasant odours or smoke while cooking. To combat this issue, perform a deep clean every few months.

- Once again, ensure that your air fryer is unplugged and cooled down before proceeding.
- Create a mix of half water and half vinegar, filling up a spray bottle.
- Remove any removable parts such as trays or baskets from the appliance.
- Spray this solution inside your air fryer—in particular around harder-to-reach nooks and crannies—and allow it to sit for roughly 10-15 minutes.
- With a soft brush or cloth, gently scrub away any stubborn food particles.
- Finally, rinse all parts thoroughly before reassembling and storing your air fryer.

3. Proper Storage- Proper storage of your air fryer is crucial in maintaining its performance. Keep the following tips in mind:

- Ensure your air fryer is fully dry before storing it, as moisture can lead to mould and bacteria.
- Store your air fryer on a flat surface, away from direct sunlight or heat sources.
- If you need to cover the appliance, using a breathable cover to prevent moisture build-up is recommended.

4. Regular Checks- Inspect your air fryer regularly for any signs of wear or damage. Check the power cord for fraying, and look for any indication of malfunction within the device. If you notice any issues, consult your user manual or contact the manufacturer for guidance.
By following these tips and best practices, you can enjoy delicious, health-conscious meals for years to come.

BREAKFAST RECIPES

British Bacon & Egg Baskets

Preparation time: 10 minutes
Cooking time: 15 minutes
Servings: 4

Ingredients:
- Eight rashers of British back bacon
- Four big British free-range eggs
- Salt & pepper, as required

Directions:
1. Warm up your air fryer to 180°C.
2. Use bacon rashers to line four silicone muffin cups, forming baskets.
3. Put egg into each bacon-lined cup, taking care not to break the yolk. Flavour with salt plus pepper.
4. Place filled muffin cups into your cooking basket, ensuring they are evenly spaced apart. Cook within 15 mins till egg whites are firm. Serve.

Nutritional Values: Calories: 289; Carbs: 1g; Fat: 21g; Protein: 23g

French Toast Stuffed Croissants

Preparation time: 15 minutes
Cooking time: 8 minutes
Servings: 4

Ingredients:
- Four croissants
- Two big eggs
- 120ml double cream
- 60g caster sugar
- One tsp vanilla extract
- Half tsp ground cinnamon
- Salt, as required
- Four tbsp Nutella or other chocolate spread
- Icing sugar, for dusting

Directions:
1. Warm up your air fryer to 180°C. Slice croissants lengthwise to create a pocket but do not cut all way through.
2. whisk eggs, double cream, caster sugar, vanilla extract, cinnamon, plus salt in your medium container.
3. Spread a generous tablespoon of Nutella inside each croissant. Gently dip each stuffed croissant in egg mixture.
4. Lightly grease your cooking basket using oil.
5. Put stuffed croissants in your cooking basket, then cook within 8 mins at 180°C till golden brown. Remove, cool it down, then dust using icing sugar. Serve.

Nutritional Values: Calories: 437; Carbs: 50g; Fat: 24g; Protein: 9g

Dutch Baby Pancake

Preparation time: 10 minutes
Cooking time: 18-20 minutes
Servings: 2-3
Ingredients:

- 120ml whole milk
- 100g plain flour
- Three big eggs
- One tbsp caster sugar
- Salt, as required
- One tsp pure vanilla extract
- Two tbsp unsalted butter, dissolved
- Icing sugar, for dusting

Directions:
1. In your container, mix milk, flour, eggs, caster sugar, salt, plus vanilla extract till smooth. Pour half butter, then mix well. Allow batter to rest within 5 mins.
2. Warm up your air fryer to 200°C, then coat using rest of butter.
3. Pour batter into your greased basket, then gently spread it out. Cook pancake within 18-20 mins till it has puffed up.
4. Transfer it to your serving plate, then dust using icing sugar. Serve.

Nutritional Values: Calories: 365; Carbs: 34g; Fat: 18g; Protein: 13g

Romanian Cheese Pillows

Preparation time: 20 minutes
Cooking time: 8 minutes
Servings: 6
Ingredients:

- 225g plain flour
- 75g cold unsalted butter, cubed
- 150g feta cheese, crumbled
- 125g ricotta cheese
- One big egg, beaten
- Salt & pepper, as required
- Olive oil for brushing

Directions:
1. In your big container, mix flour plus butter till mixture has a breadcrumb-like texture.
2. In your separate container, mix feta plus ricotta cheeses, then flavour it with salt plus pepper
3. Gradually pour water to form a soft dough. Knead within 5 mins on your floured surface.
4. Split dough into twelve, then roll each into a thin circle (around 8cm in diameter).
5. Put one tbsp cheese mixture onto each dough circle. Fold each circle in half over the filling to create semi-circles, then crimp edges together with your fingers.
6. Warm up your air fryer to 200°C.
7. Lightly brush cheese pillows using olive oil, then put them into your cooking basket – avoid overcrowding.
8. Cook within 8 mins till golden brown, flipping once. Serve.

Nutritional Values: Calories: 418; Carbs: 31g; Fat: 24g; Protein: 17g

Greek Yogurt and Granola Bars

Preparation time: 10 minutes
Cooking time: 20 minutes
Servings: 12 bars

Ingredients:

- 300g rolled oats
- 100g chopped nuts
- 100g dried fruit
- 75g unsweetened coconut flakes
- 60ml honey
- 60ml sunflower oil
- One tsp vanilla extract
- One-fourth tsp salt
- 200g Greek yogurt

Directions:

1. Warm up your air fryer to 180°C. Line your baking tray using paper liner, then put aside.
2. In your big container, mix rolled oats, chopped nuts, dried fruit, plus unsweetened coconut flakes.
3. In your separate small container, mix honey, sunflower oil, vanilla extract plus salt. Combine it with dry mixture.
4. Press granola mixture firmly onto your baking tray, then move it to your basket. Cook at 180°C within 20 mins till golden brown. Cool it down, then slice. Serve.

Nutritional Values: Calories: 280; Carbs: 34g; Fat: 13g; Protein: 8g

Portuguese Pastéis de Nata

Preparation time: 15 minutes + chilling time
Cooking time: 20 minutes
Servings: 12 pastéis

Ingredients:

- 250g puff pastry, chilled
- 25g plain flour
- 180ml whole milk
- 200g granulated sugar
- 60ml water
- One cinnamon stick & lemon peel
- Six egg yolks

Directions:

1. Roll out puff pastry to about 3mm thickness. Slice twelve 8cm circles, then press them into your non-stick muffin tin. Put tin in your fridge to chill within 15 mins.
2. In your saucepan, whisk flour plus a bit milk till smooth. Whisk in rest of milk slowly.
3. In your separate saucepan on moderate temp, mix sugar, water, cinnamon stick, plus lemon peel within 2 mins till it reaches a syrup-like.
4. Discard cinnamon stick plus lemon peel, then pour syrup into milk mixture, whisking. Warm up your air fryer to 200°C.
5. In your container, beat egg yolks, then whisk into milk sugar mixture till fully combined.
6. Remove muffin tin from your fridge, then fill each pastry case with custard.
7. Move filled muffin tin to your cooking basket. Cook within 18-20 mins till golden brown. Cool it down. Serve.

Nutritional Values: Calories: 233; Carbs: 33g; Fat: 10g; Protein: 4g

Swedish Hash Browns

Preparation time: 10 minutes
Cooking time: 12-15 minutes
Servings: 4

Ingredients:

- 600g potatoes, peel it & grated
- One small onion, chopped

- Two tbsp plain flour
- Half tsp of salt
- One-fourth tsp black pepper
- One tbsp vegetable oil

Directions:
1. In your big container, mix potatoes plus onion. Put plain flour, salt, plus pepper, then mix well. Warm up your air fryer to 190°C.
2. Divide, then shape potato mixture into eight hash brown patties. Brush both sides of each hash brown using vegetable oil.
3. Put hash brown patties in your cooking basket, then cook within 12-15 mins, flipping once, till golden. Serve.

Nutritional Values: Calories: 220; Carbs: 35g; Fat: 7g; Protein: 5g

Hungarian Langos

Preparation time: 1 hour
Cooking time: 10 minutes
Servings: 6

Ingredients:
- 450g plain flour
- One tsp each granulated sugar & salt
- 7g sachet of fast-action dried yeast
- 300ml lukewarm water
- Two tbsp vegetable oil

Directions:
1. In your big container, mix plain flour, granulated sugar, salt plus fast-action dried yeast. Pour lukewarm water, stirring to create a sticky dough.
2. Knead within 10 mins on your floured surface till elastic.
3. Put kneaded dough into your container, cover it using a damp cloth, then let it rise within 45 mins it has doubled in size.
4. Warm up your air fryer to 180°C. Divide risen dough into six, then roll each into ball. Flatten each ball to create thin discs.
5. Brush both sides of dough discs using vegetable oil, then put them in your cooking basket within 5 mins on each side till golden brown. Serve.

Nutritional Values: Calories: 341; Carbs: 61g; Fat: 7g; Protein: 8g

Italian Frittata Bites

Preparation time: 15 minutes
Cooking time: 12 minutes
Servings: 4

Ingredients:
- Six big eggs
- 100ml whole milk
- Salt & black pepper, as required
- One small red onion, chopped
- One medium courgette, grated
- 150g cherry tomatoes, halved
- 100g grated cheddar cheese
- Handful of fresh basil leaves, chopped
- Olive oil for greasing

Directions:
1. In your big container, whisk eggs, milk, salt plus pepper. Mix in red onion, grated courgette, cherry tomatoes, cheese plus chopped basil leaves.
2. Warm up your air fryer to 180°C. Grease your silicone egg bite mould using olive oil.

3. Pour egg mixture into your moulds, then move it into your cooking basket. Cook at 180°C within 12 mins till frittata bites are set. Serve.

Nutritional Values: Calories: 322; Carbs: 8g; Fat: 24g; Protein: 20g

Italian Breakfast Polenta Cakes

Preparation time: 15 minutes
Cooking time: 17 minutes
Servings: 4

Ingredients:
- 150g instant polenta
- 475ml water
- One tsp salt
- Two tbsp olive oil
- 100g grated Parmesan cheese
- 50g sun-dried tomatoes, chopped
- Two tsp fresh basil, chopped
- One tsp garlic powder
- ground black pepper, as required

Directions:
1. In your medium saucepan, let water boil. Pour polenta, whisking to avoid lumps. Put salt, then cook within 5 mins, stirring till polenta thickens.
2. Remove saucepan, then stir in olive oil, Parmesan cheese, sun-dried tomatoes, basil, garlic powder, plus black pepper.
3. Pour polenta mixture into your oiled square baking dish. Cool it down within 10 mins, then slice into squares.
4. Warm up your air fryer to 180°C. Put polenta cakes into your cooking basket. Cook within 12 mins till slightly golden. Serve.

Nutritional Values: Calories: 348; Carbs: 45g; Fat: 14g; Protein: 12g

Fluffy Air Fryer Crumpets

Preparation Time: 10 minutes + resting time
Cooking Time: 5 minutes
Servings: 10 crumpets

Ingredients:
- 250g strong white bread flour
- 7g fast-action dried yeast
- One tsp each of caster sugar & salt
- 300ml warm water
- Vegetable oil, for greasing

Directions:
1. In your big container, mix bread flour, yeast, caster sugar plus salt. Slowly pour warm water, stirring till smooth.
2. Cover, then place it in your warm area to rest within 45 mins till doubled in size.
3. Warm up your air fryer to 160°C. Grease it using vegetable oil.
4. Put crumpet rings into your cooking basket, then pour enough batter into each ring. Cook crumpets within 5 mins till bubbly. Serve.

Nutritional Values: Calories: 107; Carbs: 22g; Fat: 0g; Protein: 4g

French Toast Sticks

Preparation time: 10 minutes
Cooking time: 8 minutes
Servings: 4

Ingredients:
- Eight thick white bread slices, crusts removed & sliced into sticks
- Three big eggs
- 120ml whole milk
- One tsp vanilla extract
- One tbsp caster sugar
- Half tsp cinnamon, ground
- Salt, as required
- Cooking spray

Directions:
1. Warm up your air fryer to 190°C.
2. In your shallow container, whisk eggs, milk, vanilla extract, caster sugar, cinnamon, plus salt.
3. Dip each bread stick into egg mixture, then put on your tray. Grease your cooking basket using cooking spray, then put dipped bread sticks.
4. Cook within 4 mins on one side, flip sticks, then cook within 4 mins till golden brown. Serve.

Nutritional Values: Calories: 286; Carbs: 41g; Fat: 8g; Protein: 12g

Belgian Waffle Poppers

Preparation time: 10 minutes
Cooking time: 10 minutes
Servings: 4

Ingredients:
- 250g plain flour
- Two tsp baking powder
- One tbsp caster sugar
- Half tsp salt
- 475ml whole milk
- Two big eggs, separated
- 115g unsalted butter, dissolved & cooled slightly
- One tsp vanilla extract

Directions:
1. In your big container, whisk plain flour, baking powder, caster sugar, plus salt.
2. In another container, mix milk plus egg yolks. Slowly pour butter while whisking, then put vanilla extract. Combine it with dry mixture.
3. In your separate container, beat egg whites till stiff peaks. Fold it into batter.
4. Warm up your air fryer to 180°C. Spray it using cooking spray.
5. Spoon balls of batter into your cooking basket. Cook within 10 mins till poppers are golden brown. Serve.

Nutritional Values: Calories: 503; Carbs: 58g; Fat: 25g; Protein: 12g

German Apple Pancake Bites

Preparation time: 15 minutes
Cooking time: 12 minutes
Servings: 4

Ingredients:
- 120g plain flour
- 240ml milk
- Three big eggs
- One tsp vanilla extract
- Salt, as required
- One tbsp caster sugar

- Two medium apples, remove peels, core it, & chop
- 30g unsalted butter, dissolved

Directions:

1. In your big container, mix flour, milk, eggs, vanilla extract, salt plus caster sugar till smooth. Gently fold in chopped apples.
2. Warm up your air fryer to 180°C. Brush insides of a silicone mould using half of the melted butter.
3. Fill each mould about two-thirds full with the prepared batter. Cook in the preheated air fryer for approximately 12 mins till golden brown. Serve.
4. Carefully remove pancake bites from the moulds or basket and allow to cool slightly on a wire rack.

Nutritional Values: Calories: 343; Carbs: 44g; Fat: 14g; Protein: 10g

Spanish Churros & Chocolate

Preparation time: 20 minutes
Cooking time: 15 minutes
Servings: 4

Ingredients:

- 250ml water
- 50g caster sugar
- Salt, as required
- 2 tbsp vegetable oil, + extra for spraying
- 150g plain flour
- One tsp baking powder

For the chocolate dipping sauce:

- 200g dark chocolate, chopped
- 100ml double cream
- 50ml milk

Directions:

1. In your medium saucepan, warm up water, caster sugar, salt, plus vegetable oil on moderate temp; do not boil.
2. In your container, mix plain flour plus baking powder. Transfer it to boiling mixture, stirring till dough starts to form.
3. Remove, then cool it down within 5 mins. Transfer it into your piping bag with a star nozzle. Warm up your air fryer to 180°C.
4. Pipe approximately 10cm long churros onto a plate, cutting them with scissors. Lightly spray each churro with vegetable oil.
5. Carefully place the churros onto your air fryer tray ensuring there is enough room and don't overcrowd them. Cook within10 mins till golden brown.
6. To prepare chocolate sauce, heat double cream plus milk in your small saucepan on low temp till it steam. Add in the dark chocolate pieces, then mix till smooth.
7. Serve your air-fried churros accompanied by the warm chocolate dipping sauce.

Nutritional Values: Calories: 690; Carbs: 72g; Fat: 40g; Protein: 10g

Irish Potato Cakes

Preparation time: 15 minutes
Cooking time: 12 minutes
Servings: 4

Ingredients:

- 500g potatoes, peeled and cubed
- 100g plain flour
- 50g butter, melted
- Pinch of salt

- Two tbsp chopped fresh parsley
- One small onion, finely chopped
- One big egg, lightly beaten

Directions:

1. Boil your saucepan of water, put potatoes, then cook within 15 mins till tender. Strain, then cool it slightly.
2. In your big container, mash cooked potatoes till smooth. Mix in flour, melted butter, salt, parsley, and chopped onion. Mix in the beaten egg.
3. Divide it into eight, then form them into round potato cake.
4. Warm up your air fryer to 190°C. Oil your cooking basket and place four potato cakes in it.
5. Cook the potato cakes within 6 mins on each side till golden brown. Serve.

Nutritional Values: Calories: 306; Carbs: 45g; Fat: 10g; Protein: 7g

Swedish Cardamom Rolls

Preparation time: 15 minutes + rising time
Cooking time: 10-12 minutes
Servings: 12 rolls

Ingredients:

- 450g plain flour
- 50g caster sugar
- One tbsp ground cardamom
- One-fourth tsp salt
- 300ml warm milk
- 50g unsalted butter, melted
- 1 envelope (7g) active dry yeast

Filling:

- 100g unsalted butter, softened
- 75g caster sugar
- Three tsp ground cardamom

Glaze:

- 100g icing sugar
- Two tbsp milk

Directions:

1. In your big container, mix flour, sugar, ground cardamom, plus salt.
2. In a separate container, mix warm milk, melted butter, and yeast. Let it sit for about ten minutes until frothy.
3. Combine it with dry mixture till a soft dough forms. Knead the dough for about ten mins till elastic.
4. Put dough in your greased container, wrap using damp towel, the let it rise within about one hour.
5. Meanwhile, prepare filling by creaming softened butter, sugar, plus ground cardamom.
6. Roll out dough on your lightly floured surface, about 30cm x 40cm rectangle. Spread filling evenly on top.
7. Roll up dough tightly from one long edge to form a cylinder and cut it into 12 equal pieces.
8. Grease your air fryer basket with some butter or baking spray.
9. Put rolls into your cooking basket, then cook within 10-12 mins at 190°C till golden brown. Cool it down.
10. Meanwhile, whisk icing sugar plus milk. Drizzle it onto breakfast rolls. Serve.

Nutritional Values: Calories: 343; Carbs: 55g; Fat: 12g; Protein: 6g

English Muffin Breakfast Sandwiches

Preparation time: 10 minutes
Cooking time: 12 minutes
Servings: 2

Ingredients:

- Two English muffins, halved
- Four rashers of bacon, cooked and halved
- Two medium eggs
- 60g cheddar cheese, sliced
- Salt & black pepper, as required

Directions:
1. Warm up your air fryer to 180°C.
2. Put English muffin halves in your cooking basket, cut side up, then toast within 3 mins till desired crispiness is achieved. Remove, then put aside.
3. In your small greased, oven-safe dish or ramekin, crack an egg into each dish. Flavour it with salt plus black pepper.
4. Place the dishes with eggs into your cooking basket, then cook within 6-8 mins at 180°C till egg whites is set.
5. Remove dishes, then assemble your sandwiches as follows: one half of an English muffin, a slice of cheddar cheese, two halves of bacon, the cooked egg, then top with rest half of English muffin.
6. Put assembled sandwiches to your cooking basket, then cook within 1 min to melt the cheese slightly. Serve.

Nutritional Values: Calories: 410; Carbs: 31g; Fat: 22g; Protein: 27g

German Apple Pancakes

Preparation time: 10 minutes
Cooking time: 8 minutes
Servings: 2-3

Ingredients:
- 100g plain flour
- Two medium eggs, lightly beaten
- 150ml semi-skimmed milk
- Salt, as required
- One tsp vanilla extract
- One tbsp granulated sugar
- Two medium apples, peeled, cored & sliced thinly
- Zest of one lemon
- 30g unsalted butter, melted (plus more for greasing the fryer basket)

Directions:
1. In your big container, mix plain flour, eggs, milk, salt, plus vanilla extract.
2. Add granulated sugar plus lemon zest, then mix till evenly distributed. Gently fold in the apple slices to coat them with the batter.
3. Warm up your air fryer to 180°C. Lightly oil your cooking basket using melted butter.
4. Transfer half of the apple slice batter into the fryer basket in a circular shape (for one large pancake), ensuring that apple slices are distributed evenly on top.
5. Cook within 8 mins till golden brown. Remove, then repeat with remaining half of batter to make a second pancake.
6. Dust finished pancakes with powdered sugar before serving, if desired.

Nutritional Values: Calories: 395; Carbs: 58g; Fat: 15g; Protein: 10g

Danish Aebleskiver Puffs

Preparation time: 15 minutes
Cooking time: 10 minutes
Servings: 4

Ingredients:
- 175g plain flour
- One-fourth tsp bicarbonate of soda
- Half tsp cream of tartar
- One-eight tsp salt
- Two big eggs, separated

- 300ml whole milk
- Two tbsp caster sugar
- One tsp vanilla extract
- Cooking spray or a bit of vegetable oil, for greasing

Directions:

1. In your big container, mix flour, bicarbonate of soda, cream of tartar, plus salt.
2. In another container, whisk egg yolks, milk, sugar, plus vanilla extract till smooth. Combine it with dry mixture.
3. In your separate container, whip egg whites using your hand mixer till stiff peaks.
4. Fold whipped egg whites into batter till fully combined, but take care not to overmix or deflate the mixture.
5. Preheat your air fryer to 180°C. Lightly grease an aebleskiver pan or cake pop mould with cooking spray or vegetable oil.
6. Fill each hole in the mould generously with batter, leaving some space at the top for expansion.
7. Put mould into your cooking basket, then cook within 10 mins till golden brown; halfway through cooking, carefully turn over the puffs to ensure even browning. Serve.

Nutritional Values: Calories: 318; Carbs: 52g; Fat: 7g; Protein: 11g

Scottish Lorne Sausage Patties

Preparation time: 15 minutes
Cooking time: 14 minutes
Servings: 4

Ingredients:

- 500g minced beef
- 500g minced pork
- 150g breadcrumbs
- One big onion, finely chopped
- One tsp each allspice & nutmeg, ground
- Salt & pepper, as required
- Oil spray, for greasing

Directions:

1. In your big container, mix minced beef, minced pork plus breadcrumbs.
2. Add finely chopped onion, ground allspice, and ground nutmeg to the meat mixture. Flavour with salt plus pepper.
3. Using your hands or a round mould, form the mixture into sausage patties approximately 1cm thick.
4. Warm up your air fryer to 180°C. Lightly oil your cooking basket using oil spray to prevent the patties from sticking.
5. Place the formed sausage patties in your cooking basket, ensuring there is enough space between each patty for proper air circulation.
6. Cook for 14 minutes, flipping the patties at around halfway through to ensure even cooking on both sides. Serve.

Nutritional Values: Calories: 652; Carbs: 30g; Fat: 35g; Protein: 49g

POULTRY & TURKEY RECIPES

British Lemon-Thyme Chicken

Preparation time: 15 minutes
Cooking time: 25 minutes
Servings: 4

Ingredients:
- Four no bones & skin chicken breasts
- Two lemons (juice and zest)
- Two tbsp fresh thyme leaves, finely chopped
- 50ml olive oil
- One clove garlic, minced
- Salt & pepper, as required

Directions:
1. In your small container, mix lemon juice, lemon zest, chopped thyme leaves, olive oil, minced garlic, salt, plus pepper.
2. Put chicken breasts into your shallow container, pour the marinade over them, ensuring they're fully coated.
3. Refrigerate for at least 30 minutes or up to two hours for maximum flavour.
4. Warm up your air fryer to 180°C. Put marinated chicken breasts into your cooking basket.
5. Cook chicken within 25 minutes till cooked, flipping once. Serve.

Nutritional Values: Calories: 310; Carbs: 5g; Fat: 16g; Protein: 40g

Haggis-Stuffed Turkey Breast

Preparation time: 20 minutes
Cooking time: 40 minutes
Servings: 4

Ingredients:
- One big haggis (450g), crumbled
- Four turkey breast fillets (about 150g each)
- One tbsp olive oil
- Salt & ground black pepper, as required

Directions:
1. Warm up your air fryer to 180°C.
2. In your container, mix crumbled haggis, salt plus black pepper.
3. Place each turkey breast fillet on a clean work surface. Butterfly the fillets by making a horizontal incision along the length of each. Open up fillets.
4. Place one-fourth of the haggis mixture onto each prepared turkey breast fillet. Smooth out the stuffing in an even layer, leaving a small border along the edges.
5. Roll up each stuffed turkey breast tightly, starting at one end and finishing at the other. Secure with string if necessary.

6. Rub olive oil over the outside of each stuffed breast, then flavour with more salt plus black pepper.
7. Put stuffed turkey breasts in your cooking basket. Cook within 35-40 mins at 180°C till well-browned and cooked through. Cool it down, slice, then serve.

Nutritional Values: Calories: 475; Carbs: 22g; Fat: 28g; Protein: 39g

European Garlic Parmesan Wings

Preparation time: 15 minutes
Cooking time: 22 minutes
Servings: 4

Ingredients:
- 16 chicken wings
- One tsp olive oil, extra virgin
- Salt & ground black pepper, as required
- Four garlic cloves, minced
- 100g Parmesan cheese, grated
- 50g unsalted butter, melted
- One tsp Italian seasoning

Directions:
1. Warm up your air fryer to 190°C.
2. In your big container, mix chicken wings, olive oil, salt plus black pepper.
3. Arrange wings in your cooking basket without overlapping. Cook within 20 mins, shaking basket once.
4. In your separate container, mix minced garlic, grated Parmesan cheese, melted unsalted butter, plus Italian seasoning.
5. When the wings are crisp and fully cooked, transfer them to your big container. Pour garlic Parmesan sauce, then toss well.
6. Put sauced wings into your cooking basket, then cook within two mins till heated. Serve.

Nutritional Values: Calories: 467; Carbs: 2g; Fat: 36g; Protein: 34g

British Rosemary Turkey Tenderloin

Preparation time: 10 minutes
Cooking time: 25 minutes
Servings: 4

Ingredients:
- 400g turkey tenderloin
- Two tbsp olive oil
- Two fresh rosemary sprigs, chopped
- Two garlic cloves, minced
- One tsp sea salt
- Half tsp ground black pepper
- One lemon, zested & juiced

Directions:
1. In your small container, mix olive oil, chopped rosemary, minced garlic, sea salt, black pepper, plus lemon zest.
2. Rub the mixture evenly onto the turkey tenderloin, ensuring full coverage. Warm up your air fryer to 180°C.
3. Put turkey tenderloin in your cooking basket. Cook within 25 mins till browned. Cool it down. Slice the tenderloin, then serve with a drizzle of lemon juice.

Nutritional Values: Calories: 261; Carbs: 2g; Fat: 10g; Protein: 38g

Greek Lemon Marinated Drumsticks

Preparation time: 10 minutes + marinating time
Cooking time: 20 minutes
Servings: 4

Ingredients:
- Eight chicken drumsticks
- 60ml olive oil
- Zest & juice of two lemons
- Four garlic cloves, minced
- One tsp dried oregano
- One tsp dried thyme
- Half tsp of salt
- One-fourth tsp black pepper

Directions:
1. In In your big container, mix zest, lemon juice, olive oil, minced garlic, dried oregano, dried thyme, salt, plus black pepper.
2. Add chicken drumsticks, then toss well. Wrap using cling film, then refrigerate within 30 mins.
3. Warm up your air fryer to 180°C. Put marinated drumsticks in your cooking basket. Cook within 20 mins till golden, turning once. Serve.

Nutritional Values: Calories: 346; Carbs: 4g; Fat: 23g; Protein: 30g

Mustard-Marmalade Glazed Turkey

Preparation time: 20 minutes
Cooking time: 60 minutes
Servings: 6

Ingredients:
- One (about 3 kg) whole turkey, neck & giblets discarded
- Salt & black pepper, as required
- Four tbsp British mustard
- Four tbsp marmalade (preferably orange)
- Two tbsp Worcestershire sauce
- One tbsp olive oil

Directions:
1. Warm up your air fryer to 180°C.
2. Prepare the turkey by patting it dry using kitchen paper. Flavour it generously with salt plus black pepper. Don't forget the cavity!
3. In your small container, mix mustard, marmalade, and Worcestershire sauce.
4. Spread 1/2 mustard-marmalade mixture evenly over turkey, ensuring that all parts are covered.
5. Carefully place the seasoned turkey in your cooking basket. Cook within 30 mins at 180°C. Then carefully flip it over so that it is now breast-side up.
6. Brush the remaining mustard-marmalade mixture over the entire surface of the turkey.
7. Continue cooking for an additional 30 minutes till cooked. Cool it down, carve, then serve.

Nutritional Values: Calories: 620; Carbs: 12g; Fat: 24g; Protein: 86g

Italian Air Fryer Chicken Piccata

Preparation time: 15 minutes
Cooking time: 25 minutes
Servings: 4
Ingredients:
- Four no bones & skin chicken breasts (about 500g)
- 100g plain flour
- Half tsp of salt

- One-fourth tsp ground black pepper
- Two big eggs, beaten
- 200g breadcrumbs
- 75g grated Parmesan cheese
- Two tbsp olive oil
- 100ml chicken stock
- Juice of one lemon
- Two garlic cloves, minced
- One tsp capers, strained & washed
- One tbsp chopped fresh parsley

Directions:

1. In your shallow container, mix flour, salt, plus pepper. In another container, place beaten eggs. In your third container, mix breadcrumbs plus Parmesan.
2. Dip each chicken breast in flour mixture, then in beaten eggs, then finally in breadcrumb mixture.
3. Warm up your air fryer to 180°C. Brush breaded chicken breast on all sides using olive oil. Put chicken breasts in your cooking basket.
4. Air fry within 10 mins, flip, then continue cooking within 10 mins till golden brown.
5. Meanwhile, mix chicken stock, lemon juice, minced garlic, plus capers in your small saucepan on moderate temp. Simmer within 5 mins till slightly reduced.
6. To serve, plate each chicken breast and spoon some of the sauce on top.

Nutritional Values: Calories: 505; Carbs: 41g; Fat: 19g; Protein: 38g

Schnitzel-Style Turkey Breasts

Preparation time: 15 minutes
Cooking time: 12 minutes
Servings: 4

Ingredients:

- Four (about 600g) turkey breast escalopes
- 100g plain flour
- Two big eggs, beaten
- 200g panko breadcrumbs
- Salt & pepper, as required
- Olive oil spray

Directions:

1. Lay out a sheet of cling film on a clean surface.
2. Place one turkey breast escalope on the cling film, cover with another sheet of cling film, and use a rolling pin to flatten the escalope to an even 0.5cm thickness. Repeat for the remaining turkey breasts and set aside.
3. Set up three shallow dishes for coating the turkey escalopes. In first dish, place the flour seasoned with salt plus pepper.
4. In the second dish, beat eggs. In third dish, add the panko breadcrumbs.
5. One at a time, coat each turkey escalope in flour, shaking off any excess, then dip it in beaten egg, then finally press it into the panko breadcrumbs to coat evenly.
6. Warm up your air fryer to 180°C.
7. Place two coated turkey breasts in your cooking basket. Lightly spray with olive oil spray.
8. Cook turkey breasts within 6 mins at 180°C, flip them, then cook within 6 mins till golden brown. Serve.

Nutritional Values: Calories: 485; Carbs: 48g; Fat: 12g; Protein: 43g

French Provencal Chicken Thighs

Preparation time: 10 minutes
Cooking time: 20 minutes
Servings: 4

Ingredients:

- Eight (~1.2 kg) chicken thighs, bone-in and skin-on
- Two garlic cloves, minced
- One tbsp each dried oregano, rosemary & thyme
- Zest of one lemon
- Juice of half lemon
- Salt & ground black pepper, as required
- Olive oil spray

Directions:

1. In your small container, mix minced garlic, oregano, rosemary, thyme, zest, plus lemon juice.
2. Place chicken thighs in your big container. Flavour with salt plus black pepper.
3. Pour marinade over chicken thighs, then rub it in well to ensure each piece is covered. Marinate for at least 20 minutes or up to overnight.
4. Warm up your air fryer to180°C. Oil your cooking basket using olive oil spray.
5. Arrange marinated chicken thighs in your basket. Cook at 180°C within 20 mins, turning once. Cool it down. Serve.

Nutritional Values: Calories: 450; Carbs: 3g; Fat: 30g; Protein: 42g

Irish Orange Infused Turkey Breast

Preparation time: 15 minutes + marinating time
Cooking time: 45 minutes
Servings: 4

Ingredients:

- 800g turkey breast, boneless and skinless
- One big orange, zested and juiced
- Two tbsp olive oil
- Three garlic cloves, minced
- One tbsp each fresh rosemary & thyme, chopped
- Salt & ground black pepper, as required

Directions:

1. In your small container, mix orange zest, orange juice, olive oil, minced garlic, rosemary, thyme, salt, plus black pepper.
2. Put turkey breast in your shallow container, then pour marinade over it. Cover then refrigerate within 1 hour.
3. Warm up your air fryer to 180°C.
4. Remove marinated turkey breast, then pat dry using paper towels. Reserve marinade for later use.
5. Put turkey breast in your cooking basket, then cook within 45 mins till cooked.
6. Baste with reserved marinade every 15 minutes for extra flavour. Cool it down. Slice, then serve.

Nutritional Values: Calories: 428; Carbs: 6g; Fat: 16g; Protein: 61g

British Turkey & Cranberry Fritters

Preparation time: 15 minutes
Cooking time: 12 minutes
Servings: 4

Ingredients:

- 200g cooked turkey, shredded
- 100g dried cranberries, chopped
- One medium onion, chopped
- 100g plain flour

- Half tsp baking powder
- One tsp dried mixed herbs
- One big egg, beaten
- Salt & pepper, as required
- Olive oil spray

Directions:

1. In your big container, mix shredded turkey, chopped cranberries, plus finely chopped onion.
2. In your separate container, whisk plain flour, baking powder, plus dried mixed herbs. Combine it with turkey mixture.
3. Add beaten egg, then stir till it forms a thick batter. Flavour using salt plus pepper.
4. Warm up your air fryer to 180°C. Spray your cooking basket using olive oil spray.
5. Use your hands or a spoon to form small fritters from the batter, then put them in your cooking basket.
6. Cook within 12 mins till golden brown, turning once. Cool it down. Slice, then serve.

Nutritional Values: Calories: 280; Carbs: 34g; Fat: 6g; Protein: 20g

Hungarian Paprika Chicken Tenders

Preparation time: 10 minutes
Cooking time: 12 minutes
Servings: 4

Ingredients:

- 500g chicken tenders
- One tbsp Hungarian paprika
- One tsp garlic powder
- Half tsp each onion powder, thyme & salt
- One-fourth tsp black pepper
- Cooking spray

Directions:

1. In your small container, mix Hungarian paprika, garlic powder, onion powder, thyme, salt, plus black pepper.
2. Pat the chicken tenders dry using paper towel, then put them in your big container.
3. Sprinkle the spice blend over the chicken tenders, ensuring that each piece is evenly coated with the mixture.
4. Warm up your air fryer to 180°C. Spray your cooking basket using cooking spray.
5. Arrange seasoned chicken tenders in your cooking basket. Cook within 12 mins, turning once till golden brown. Serve.

Nutritional Values: Calories: 215; Carbs: 2g; Fat: 5g; Protein: 38g

Herb de Provence Roasted Turkey Legs

Preparation time: 15 minutes
Cooking time: 25 minutes
Servings: 4

Ingredients:

- Four turkey legs
- Two tbsp olive oil
- Three tsp Herb de Provence
- Half tsp of salt
- One-fourth tsp black pepper
- Two garlic cloves, minced
- Zest of one lemon

Directions:

1. In your small container, mix olive oil, Herb de Provence, salt, black pepper, minced garlic plus lemon zest to create a marinade.

2. Pat turkey legs dry using kitchen paper, then coat with marinade. Let them rest for at least 10 minutes to allow the flavours to infuse.
3. Warm up your air fryer to 190°C. Put marinated turkey legs in your cooking basket. Cook turkey legs within 25-30 mins till cooked. Serve.

Nutritional Values: Calories: 480; Carbs: 2g; Fat: 22g; Protein: 62g

Dutch Creamy Mustard Chicken Wings

Preparation time: 15 minutes
Cooking time: 25 minutes
Servings: 4

Ingredients:
- One kg chicken wings
- Two tbsp Dijon mustard
- 150 ml double cream
- One small onion, finely chopped
- Two garlic cloves, minced
- 60 ml white wine (optional)
- Two tsp wholegrain mustard
- Salt & black pepper, as required

Directions:
1. In your medium container, mix Dijon mustard, double cream, onion, garlic cloves, white wine (if using), wholegrain mustard, salt, plus black pepper.
2. Add chicken wings to the marinade and ensure they are evenly coated. Cover, then refrigerate within one hour.
3. Warm up your air fryer to 180°C. Once marinated, arrange chicken wings in your air fryer basket.
4. Cook wings within 25 mins, turning them once till browned.
5. Once fully cooked, put chicken wings onto your serving plate and drizzle them with any remaining marinade from the bowl. Serve.

Nutritional Values: Calories: 530; Carbs: 4g; Fat: 28g; Protein: 40g

Zesty Italian Turkey Cutlets

Preparation time: 20 minutes
Cooking time: 25 minutes
Servings: 4

Ingredients:
- Four turkey cutlets, about 150g each
- 100g Italian breadcrumbs
- One tsp garlic powder
- One tbsp chopped fresh parsley
- Half tsp salt
- One-fourth tsp black pepper
- Two eggs, beaten
- 75g plain flour
- Cooking spray

Directions:
1. Warm up your air fryer to 190°C.
2. In your shallow container, mix breadcrumbs, garlic powder, parsley, salt plus pepper.
3. Place beaten eggs in your separate shallow container and flour in another.
4. Dredge turkey cutlets in flour, dip into beaten eggs, ensuring that both sides are coated. Lastly, coat both sides with the breadcrumb mixture.
5. Spray your cooking basket using cooking spray, ensuring it's well-greased for non-stick purposes.

6. Put breaded turkey cutlets into your cooking basket without overcrowding them. Lightly spray each cutlet using cooking spray.
7. Cook within 20-25 mins till golden brown, turning once. Serve.

Nutritional Values: Calories: 450; Carbs: 35g; Fat: 15g; Protein: 40g

Souvlaki Chicken Skewers

Preparation time: 10 minutes + marinating time
Cooking time: 15 minutes
Servings: 4

Ingredients:
- Four no bones & skin chicken breasts, sliced into 2 cm cubes
- Two garlic cloves, minced
- 125 ml Greek yoghurt
- 30 ml lemon juice
- 30 ml olive oil
- One tbsp dried oregano
- Salt & ground black pepper, as required

Directions:
1. In your big container, whisk garlic, Greek yoghurt, lemon juice, olive oil, oregano, salt plus black pepper.
2. Add chicken cubes, then mix till well coated. Cover, then refrigerate within 1 hour.
3. Warm up your air fryer to 200°C. Thread marinated chicken cubes onto your soaked skewers, leaving some space between each cube.
4. Place the chicken skewers in a single layer in your cooking basket, then cook within 10 mins.
5. Flip skewers, then cook within 5 mins till cooked through. Serve.

Nutritional Values: Calories: 244; Carbs: 2g; Fat: 12g; Protein: 29g

Spanish Style Turkey Meatballs

Preparation time: 15 minutes
Cooking time: 21 minutes
Servings: 4

Ingredients:
- 500g turkey mince
- One small onion, finely chopped
- Two garlic cloves, minced
- 50g breadcrumbs
- One big egg
- One tsp smoked paprika
- Half tsp cumin
- Salt & pepper, as required
- Olive oil spray

For the sauce:
- Two tbsp olive oil
- One small onion, finely chopped
- One garlic clove, minced
- 400g canned chopped tomatoes
- Pinch of sugar
- Salt & pepper, as required

Directions:
1. In your big container, mix turkey mince, onion, garlic, breadcrumbs, egg, smoked paprika, cumin, salt plus pepper.
2. Shape it into golf ball-sized meatballs, then put them aside.
3. Warm up your air fryer to 180°C. Lightly spray your meatballs using olive oil spray, then put them in your cooking basket. Cook within 10 mins till golden brown.

4. Meanwhile, warm up olive oil in your saucepan on moderate temp. Add onion, then cook till softened. Add garlic, then cook within 1 min.
5. Stir in canned tomatoes, sugar, salt plus pepper. Let it simmer, then cook within 10 mins. Add meatballs, then gently mix. Serve.

Nutritional Values: Calories: 265; Carbs: 16g; Fat: 12g; Protein: 22g

Peri Peri Chicken Strips

Preparation time: 10 minutes
Cooking time: 15 minutes
Servings: 4

Ingredients:
- 500g chicken breast, cut into strips
- 100ml Nando's Peri Peri sauce (choose your preferred spice level)
- Two tbsp olive oil
- 50g plain flour
- One tsp each paprika & garlic powder
- Salt & black pepper, as required

Directions:
1. In your small container, mix Peri Peri sauce plus olive oil. Put aside.
2. In your separate shallow container, mix flour, paprika, garlic powder, salt, plus black pepper.
3. Dip each chicken strip into Peri Peri sauce mixture, ensuring they are well-coated.
4. Next, coat the chicken strips in the flour mixture, pressing down to ensure they are evenly covered.
5. Warm up your air fryer to 180°C. Put coated chicken strips into your cooking basket, then cook within 15 mins till golden brown. Serve.

Nutritional Values: Calories: 310; Carbs: 12g; Fat: 11g; Protein: 39g

French Tarragon-Roasted Turkey Thighs

Preparation time: 10 minutes
Cooking time: 25 minutes
Servings: 4

Ingredients:
- Four (approximately 1.5kg) turkey thighs, pat dried
- Two tbsp olive oil
- One tbsp dried tarragon
- Zest & juice of one British lemon
- Two garlic cloves, minced
- Salt &ground black pepper, as required

Directions:
1. Warm up your air fryer to 180°C.
2. In your small container, mix olive oil, dried tarragon, zest, lemon juice, minced garlic, salt, plus black pepper.
3. Put turkey thighs on your big plate. Rub tarragon mixture evenly on the turkey thighs, ensuring they are well coated.
4. Arrange seasoned turkey thighs in your cooking basket. Cook within 25 mins till golden brown. Serve.

Nutritional Values: Calories: 485; Carbs: 2g; Fat: 22g; Protein: 65g

Swedish Crispy Chicken Meatballs

Preparation time: 15 minutes
Cooking time: 20 minutes
Servings: 4

Ingredients:
- 500g minced chicken
- 75g fresh breadcrumbs
- One small onion, finely chopped
- One garlic clove, minced
- One tsp dried parsley
- Half tsp each ground allspice & nutmeg
- Salt & pepper, as required
- Two tbsp vegetable oil

Directions:
1. In your big container, mix minced chicken, breadcrumbs, onion, garlic, parsley, allspice, nutmeg, salt plus pepper. Using clean hands or a spoon, form into small meatballs.
2. Warm up your air fryer to 180°C. Lightly coat your cooking basket using vegetable oil. Put meatballs in your cooking basket.
3. Cook within 10 mins, flip meatballs, then cook within10 mins till golden brown. Serve.

Nutritional Values: Calories: 315; Carbs: 8g; Fat: 20g; Protein: 24g

Buffalo Fried Turkey Nuggets

Preparation time: 15 minutes
Cooking time: 12 minutes
Servings: 4

Ingredients:
- 500g turkey breast, cut into bite-sized nuggets
- 240ml buffalo sauce
- 240ml panko breadcrumbs
- 120g plain flour
- Two big free-range eggs, beaten
- Salt & black pepper, as required
- Cooking spray

Directions:
1. In your shallow container, mix flour, salt plus black pepper.
2. Put beaten eggs plus panko breadcrumbs in two separate shallow containers.
3. Coat each turkey nugget in seasoned flour, dip it into beaten eggs, then coat it with panko breadcrumbs. Ensure each nugget is well-coated. Set aside on a plate.
4. Warm up your air fryer to 180°C. Lightly oil your cooking basket using cooking spray.
5. Put breaded turkey nuggets in your cooking basket. Cook within 10-12 mins, flipping once till golden brown.
6. In your microwave-safe container, warm up buffalo sauce within 30 seconds.
7. Toss the cooked turkey nuggets in the buffalo sauce until evenly coated. Serve immediately with your favourite blue cheese or ranch dipping sauce.

Nutritional Values: Calories: 382; Carbs: 36g; Fat: 10g; Protein: 37g

BEEF, PORK AND LAMB

Garlic Herb Beef Tenderloin

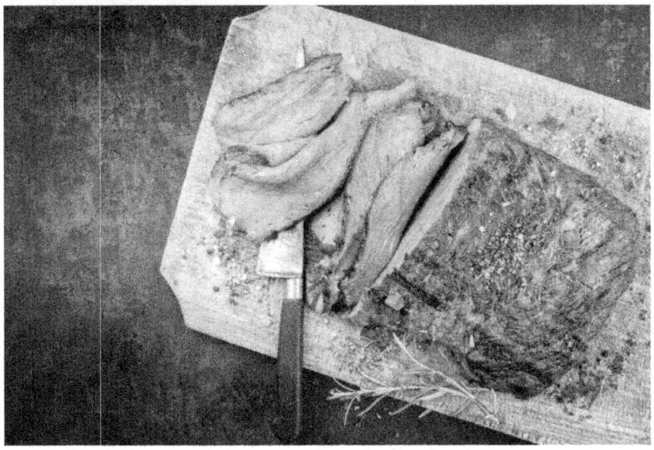

Preparation time: 10 minutes
Cooking time: 25 minutes
Servings: 4
Ingredients:
- 800g beef tenderloin, trimmed
- One tbsp olive oil
- Four garlic cloves, minced
- One tsp each rosemary & thyme, dried
- Half tsp each sea salt & ground black pepper

Directions:
1. In a small container, mix minced garlic, dried rosemary, dried thyme, sea salt, plus black pepper.
2. Drizzle beef tenderloin using olive oil, then rub garlic herb mixture all over the tenderloin.
3. Warm up your air fryer to 190°C.
4. Put seasoned beef tenderloin in your cooking basket, then cook within 25 mins, turning once. Cool it down.
5. Slice the rested beef tenderloin into thin slices and serve with your favourite side dishes.

Nutritional Values: Calories: 420; Carbs: 2g; Fat: 28g; Protein: 40g

Irish Corned Beef Hash Patties

Preparation time: 15 minutes
Cooking time: 20 minutes
Servings: 4

Ingredients:
- 400g canned corned beef, drained & crumbled
- 450g cold mashed potatoes
- One small onion, chopped
- One tsp Worcestershire sauce
- One-fourth tsp ground black pepper
- 100g sharp Cheddar cheese, grated
- Two big eggs, beaten
- 200g breadcrumbs
- Olive oil spray for the air fryer

Directions:
1. In your big container, mix crumbled corned beef, mashed potatoes, onion, Worcestershire sauce, plus black pepper.
2. Divide it into eight, then shape each into a round patty.
3. Place some grated Cheddar cheese on top of four patties, then top it with another patty. Ensure that the edges are sealed properly.
4. Prepare a breading station with two shallow plates, one with beaten eggs and the other with breadcrumbs.
5. Dip each patty into the egg, ensuring it's fully coated before transferring it onto the breadcrumbs. Press gently so that the breadcrumbs adhere properly.
6. Preheat an air fryer at 180°C for around five minutes. Lightly oil your air fryer basket using olive oil spray.
7. Put patties in your cooking basket without overlapping. Cook for ten minutes before flipping them over gently and cooking for another ten mins till golden brown. Serve.

Nutritional Values: Calories: 520; Carbs: 44g; Fat: 25g; Protein: 28g

Beef and Mushroom Stroganoff Bites

Preparation time: 15 minutes
Cooking time: 15 minutes
Servings: 4

Ingredients:

- 500g lean beef steak, sliced into bite-sized pieces
- 250g chestnut mushrooms, sliced
- One small onion, chopped
- Two garlic cloves, minced
- 150ml beef stock
- 100ml double cream
- Two tbsp olive oil
- One tbsp Worcestershire sauce
- Salt & black pepper, as required

Directions:

1. In your container, mix beef steak pieces, 1 tbsp olive oil, minced garlic, salt, plus pepper. Put aside within 10 mins.
2. Warm up your air fryer to 200°C.
3. In your pan on moderate temp, add rest of olive oil, then sauté chopped onions till translucent.
4. Add the mushrooms to the pan, then cook till they are softened.
5. Place the marinated beef and mushroom mixture in your cooking basket. Cook within 8 mins, shaking basket once.
6. In your separate pan on low temp, mix beef stock, double cream, and Worcestershire sauce. Let it simmer.
7. Add cooked beef plus mushroom mixture. Stir well, then cook within 4 mins. Flavour with salt plus black pepper. Serve.

Nutritional Values: Calories: 396; Carbs: 7g; Fat: 27g; Protein: 32g

Air Fried Beef Schnitzel

Preparation time: 15 minutes
Cooking time: 10 minutes
Servings: 4

Ingredients:

- Four thin beef schnitzel slices (about 600g)
- 100g plain flour
- Half tsp salt
- One-fourth tsp black pepper
- Two medium beaten free-range eggs
- 150g breadcrumbs
- Cooking spray

Directions:

1. Warm up your air fryer to 200°C.
2. Prepare three shallow dishes: one with flour mixed with salt plus black pepper, another with beaten eggs, and a third one with breadcrumbs.
3. Dredge each beef schnitzel slice in flour mixture, then egg, and finally coating it with breadcrumbs, pressing gently to make sure the breadcrumbs adhere.
4. Place each coated schnitzel onto a plate or tray to rest for a couple of minutes before frying.
5. Lightly oil schnitzels on all sides using cooking spray, then put them in your cooking basket.
6. Cook within five mins on one side, then carefully flip the schnitzels over using tongs and continue cooking for an additional five mins till golden brown. Serve.

Nutritional Values: Calories: 459; Carbs: 32g; Fat: 12g; Protein: 51g

Tuscan-Style Beef Steak

Preparation time: 10 minutes + marinating time
Cooking time: 12 minutes
Servings: 4

Ingredients:

- Four beef steaks (approximately 150g each)
- Four tbsp olive oil
- Two tbsp balsamic vinegar
- Two garlic cloves, minced
- Zest and juice of half a lemon
- Two tsp rosemary, dried
- One tsp oregano, dried
- Salt & pepper, as required

Directions:

1. In your small container, mix olive oil, balsamic vinegar, minced garlic, lemon zest and juice, rosemary, oregano, salt, plus pepper.
2. Put steaks in your big container, then pour marinade over them. Cover with clingfilm, then chill within one hour in your fridge.
3. Warm up your air fryer to 200°C.
4. Transfer marinated steaks into your cooking basket. Make sure not to overlap them or let them touch each other.
5. Cook for six minutes, then flip each steak over, then cook within six mins till cooked through. Serve.

Nutritional Values: Calories: 406; Carbs: 2g; Fat: 27g; Protein: 37g

Beef and Potato Croquettes

Preparation time: 20 minutes
Cooking time: 15 minutes
Servings: 4

Ingredients:

- 450g minced beef
- 500g potatoes, peeled & diced
- One small onion, chopped
- Two garlic cloves, minced
- Two tbsp chopped parsley
- One big egg, beaten
- 75g plain flour
- 100g breadcrumbs, preferably panko
- Salt & pepper, as required
- Olive oil spray

Directions:

1. Put diced potatoes in your pot filled with cold water. Let it boil, then cook within 10 mins till tender. Strain and return potatoes to your pot. Mash the potatoes until smooth and allow them to cool.
2. In your big container, mix minced beef, onion, garlic, parsley, salt, plus pepper. Mix in cooled mashed potatoes.
3. Shape it into small croquettes (about size of golf balls).
4. Prepare three shallow dishes: one with flour, one with beaten egg, and one with breadcrumbs. Roll each croquette first in flour, then dip in egg, followed by rolling in breadcrumbs.
5. Warm up air fryer to 200°C. Put breaded croquettes into your cooking basket. Lightly oil croquettes with olive oil spray.
6. Cook within 15 mins till golden brown, shaking basket once. Serve.

Nutritional Values: Calories: 612; Carbs: 56g; Fat: 19g; Protein: 45g

Budapest Beef Paprika Bites

Preparation time: 15 minutes
Cooking time: 12 minutes
Servings: 4

Ingredients:

- 500g lean beef mince
- 60g finely chopped onion
- One garlic clove, minced
- Two tbsp tomato purée
- One tbsp each plain flour & paprika
- One tsp caraway seeds, crushed
- Salt & pepper, as required
- Olive oil spray

Directions:

1. In your big container, mix beef mince, chopped onion, garlic, tomato purée, flour, paprika, crushed caraway seeds, salt plus pepper. Shape it into 16 evenly-sized bites.
2. Warm up your air fryer to 200°C. Lightly spray each beef bite with olive oil, then put them in your cooking basket.
3. Cook within 6 mins, flip each bite, then cook within 6 mins till golden. Serve.

Nutritional Values: Calories: 321; Carbs: 7g; Fat: 20g; Protein: 28g

Irish Bacon and Cabbage

Preparation time: 15 minutes
Cooking time: 30 minutes
Servings: 4

Ingredients:

- 500g back bacon, diced
- One small head of cabbage, shredded
- One big onion, chopped
- Two garlic cloves, minced
- 300ml chicken stock
- Two tbsp vegetable oil
- Salt & pepper, as required

Directions:

1. Warm up your air fryer to 180°C.
2. In your big container, mix diced bacon plus vegetable oil.
3. Put bacon into your cooking basket, then cook within 10 mins, shaking basket once.
4. In your same container, mix shredded cabbage, chopped onion plus minced garlic. Flavour with salt plus pepper.
5. After initial 10 minutes of cooking the bacon, carefully remove your cooking basket, then add cabbage mixture.
6. Cook within 15 mins till cabbage is tender, shaking occasionally for even cooking.
7. Meanwhile, warm up chicken stock in your saucepan on moderate temp till warmed through.
8. Transfer bacon and cabbage to your serving dish. Pour warm chicken stock over it and stir gently to combine all ingredients evenly.
9. Serve immediately alongside your favourite Irish soda bread or as a standalone dish.

Nutritional Values: Calories: 399; Carbs: 14g; Fat: 27g; Protein: 28g

British Air Fried Bangers

Preparation time: 10 minutes
Cooking time: 12 minutes
Servings: 4

Ingredients:

- Eight British bangers (pork sausages)
- One tbsp rapeseed oil
- One tsp each dried sage & thyme
- Salt & pepper, as required

Directions:

1. Warm up your air fryer to 190°C.
2. In your big container, mix rapeseed oil, dried sage, dried thyme, salt, plus pepper. Add bangers, then gently toss them.
3. Arrange bangers in your cooking basket. Cook within 12 mins till golden brown, turning them once. Serve.
4. Once cooked, carefully remove the bangers from the air fryer and let them rest for a few minutes on a plate.

Nutritional Values: Calories: 460; Carbs: 2g; Fat: 36g; Protein: 30g

Pork Souvlaki in Pita Bread

Preparation time: 15 minutes
Cooking time: 10 minutes
Servings: 4

Ingredients:

- 500g lean pork tenderloin, cubed
- Four pita breads, warmed
- One big red onion, sliced into wedges
- One green bell pepper, sliced into chunks
- Two tbsp extra-virgin olive oil
- Juice of one lemon
- Two garlic cloves, minced
- One tsp dried oregano
- Salt & black pepper, as required

For Tzatziki sauce:

- 150g Greek yogurt
- Half cucumber, grated and drained well
- One garlic clove, minced
- One tsp white wine vinegar
- Salt & black pepper, as required

Directions:

1. In your container, mix pork cubes, olive oil, lemon juice, garlic, oregano, salt, plus black pepper. Marinate within 30 mins.
2. Warm up your air fryer to 180°C. Thread marinated pork cubes onto skewers along with onion wedges and green bell pepper. Discard any remaining marinade.
3. Cook skewers in your air fryer within 10 mins till pork is cooked through.
4. While the skewers cook, prepare the tzatziki sauce by combining all sauce fixings in your container till smooth.
5. To assemble your pork souvlaki in pita bread, spread a generous amount of tzatziki down the centre of each warmed pita bread.
6. Remove the cooked pork and vegetables from the skewers and layer them on top of the tzatziki sauce.
7. Fold the pita bread around the fillings, then serve immediately along with extra tzatziki sauce on the side.

Nutritional Values: Calories: 598; Carbs: 36g; Fat: 25g; Protein: 59g

Pork and Apple Skewers

Preparation time: 15 minutes
Cooking time: 12 minutes
Servings: 4

Ingredients:

- 500g pork tenderloin, sliced into 2cm cubes

- Two medium apples, cored and sliced into 2cm pieces
- One red onion, cut into wedges
- Two tbsp olive oil
- One tsp paprika
- Salt & black pepper, as required

Directions:
1. In your big container, mix cubed pork, apple pieces plus onion wedges. Add olive oil, paprika, salt plus pepper. Toss well.
2. Warm up your air fryer to 180°C.
3. Thread the marinated pork, apples and onions onto the skewers, alternating between each ingredient.
4. Put prepared skewers in your cooking basket.
5. Cook within 6 mins, then carefully turn the skewers over using tongs or a fork, then cook within 6 mins till pork is cooked through. Serve.

Nutritional Values: Calories: 310; Carbs: 15g; Fat: 12g; Protein: 35g

Spanish Chorizo Pork Sausages

Preparation time: 10 minutes
Cooking time: 15 minutes
Servings: 4

Ingredients:
- 450g UK Spanish Chorizo Pork Sausages
- One tbsp olive oil
- One tsp smoked paprika
- Half tsp garlic powder
- Salt & black pepper, as required

Directions:
1. In your small container, mix olive oil, smoked paprika, garlic powder, salt, plus pepper.
2. Put sausages in your big container, then pour spice mixture over them. Toss well.
3. Warm up your air fryer to 180°C.
4. Arrange the seasoned sausages in your cooking basket. Cook within 15 mins, flipping once. Serve.

Nutritional Values: Calories: 323; Carbs: 1g; Fat: 24g; Protein: 21g

Belgian Pork Belly Tidbits

Preparation time: 15 minutes
Cooking time: 25 minutes
Servings: 4

Ingredients:
- 500g pork belly, sliced into small chunks
- Two tbsp olive oil
- One tsp garlic powder
- One tsp onion powder
- Salt & black pepper, as required
- 125ml Belgian beer (Alternatively, use a UK Pale Ale)
- Two tbsp wholegrain mustard
- Two tbsp honey

Directions:
1. In your big container, mix pork belly chunks with the olive oil, garlic & onion powder, salt, plus pepper.
2. Warm up your air fryer to 190°C.
3. Put seasoned pork belly pieces in your cooking basket. Cook within 20 mins till crisp, shaking basket once.

4. Meanwhile, in your saucepan on moderate-low temp, mix Belgian beer, wholegrain mustard, plus honey together. Stir occasionally until well combined.
5. Remove the cooked pork belly tidbits from the air fryer, then put them in your big container.
6. Pour beer-mustard mixture over cooked pork tidbits and toss gently to coat. Serve.

Nutritional Values: Calories: 590; Carbs: 10g; Fat: 46g; Protein: 30g

Spicy Harissa Leg of Lamb

Preparation time: 20 minutes
Cooking time: 1 hour
Servings: 6

Ingredients:
- 1.5 kg leg of lamb, deboned and butterflied
- 100 g harissa paste
- Three garlic cloves, minced
- Juice of one lemon
- Two tbsp olive oil
- Salt & ground black pepper, as required

Directions:
1. In your small container, mix harissa paste, minced garlic, lemon juice, plus olive
2. Lay the butterflied leg of lamb on a cutting board with the inside facing up. Flavour with salt plus black pepper.
3. Spread harissa mixture evenly over inside surface of lamb.
4. Roll up the lamb tightly and tie it with butcher's twine in several places to maintain its shape. Warm up your air fryer to 180°C.
5. Place rolled leg of lamb into your cooking basket. Cook within 1 hour till cooked through. If you prefer medium or well done, increase cooking time accordingly while monitoring the internal temperature.
6. Once cooked, carefully remove the leg of lamb from the air fryer using heat-resistant gloves or tongs.
7. Let the cooked leg of lamb rest for about 10 minutes before slicing. Serve.

Nutritional Values: Calories: 438; Carbs: 4g; Fat: 28g; Protein: 40g

Crispy Italian Lamb Chops

Preparation time: 15 minutes
Cooking time: 20 minutes
Servings: 4

Ingredients:
- Eight lamb chops
- 100g Italian breadcrumbs
- Two tbsp grated Parmesan cheese
- Two tsp dried oregano
- One tsp each garlic powder & onion powder
- Salt & ground black pepper, as required
- Two big eggs, beaten
- Olive oil spray

Directions:
1. In your shallow container, mix Italian breadcrumbs, Parmesan cheese, dried oregano, garlic & onion powder, salt, plus black pepper. In another shallow container, beat the eggs.
2. Warm up your air fryer to 190°C.

3. Dip lamb chops into beaten egg mixture, ensuring they are fully coated. Then press each chop into the breadcrumb mixture to coat both sides evenly.
4. Place the breaded lamb chops onto a plate as you work on the others.
5. Once all lamb chops are breaded, spray them using olive oil spray.
6. Arrange lamb chops in your cooking basket. Do not overcrowd the basket; cook in batches if necessary.
7. Cook for 10 mins, then carefully flip the chops using tongs, then cook within 10 mins till golden brown. Serve.

Nutritional Values: Calories: 461; Carbs: 16g; Fat: 24g; Protein: 42g

Rosemary Garlic Lamb Racks

Preparation time: 15 minutes + marinating time
Cooking time: 15-20 minutes
Servings: 4

Ingredients:
- Two lamb racks (approx. 700g each), trimmed
- Two tbsp olive oil
- Three garlic cloves, minced
- Two tbsp fresh rosemary, chopped
- One tsp sea salt
- Half tsp black pepper, ground
- Zest of one lemon

Directions:
1. In your small container, mix olive oil, minced garlic, rosemary, sea salt, black pepper, plus lemon zest to create the marinade.
2. Rub the marinade evenly onto the lamb racks, ensuring full coverage. Let it marinate within 1 hour in your fridge.
3. Warm up your air fryer to 180°C.
4. Put marinated lamb racks in your cooking basket with bones facing downwards.
5. Cook within 15 mins if you like medium rare or 20 mins for medium to well-done. Cool it down, slice, then serve.

Nutritional Values: Calories: 620; Carbs: 2g; Fat: 44g; Protein: 48g

Greek Style Lamb Meatballs

Preparation time: 15 minutes + chilling time
Cooking time: 15 minutes
Servings: 4

Ingredients:
500g minced lamb
- One small red onion, finely chopped
- Three garlic cloves, minced
- 100g feta cheese, crumbled
- 50g breadcrumbs
- One big egg, beaten
- Two tbsp each fresh mint & parsley leaves, chopped
- One tsp each dried oregano & paprika
- Salt & ground black pepper, as required
- Olive oil for drizzling (optional)

Directions:
1. In your big container, mix minced lamb, chopped red onion, minced garlic, crumbled feta cheese, breadcrumbs, beaten egg, chopped mint and parsley leaves, dried oregano, paprika, salt and pepper. Mix well until all ingredients are evenly distributed.

2. Roll the mixture into golf ball-sized meatballs and place them on a plate. Refrigerate for at least 30 minutes to firm up the meatballs.
3. Warm up your air fryer to 180°C. Lightly oil your cooking basket using olive oil.
4. Put meatballs in your cooking basket, then cook within 15 mins till cooked through, flipping them once. Serve.

Nutritional Values: Calories: 457; Carbs: 22g; Fat: 32g; Protein: 29g

Sizzling Spiced Lamb Pinchos

Preparation time: 15 minutes + marinating time
Cooking time: 10 minutes
Servings: 4

Ingredients:
- 500g diced lamb leg
- Two garlic cloves, minced
- One tbsp each smoked paprika, ground cumin & coriander
- Half tsp chilli flakes
- Zest & juice of one lemon
- Three tbsp olive oil
- Salt & ground black pepper, as required

Directions:
1. In your big container, mix minced garlic, smoked paprika, ground cumin, ground coriander, chilli flakes, lemon zest & juice, olive oil, salt, plus pepper.
2. Add the diced lamb leg to the spice paste, making sure each piece is fully coated. Cover, then marinate in your fridge within one hour.
3. Warm up your air fryer to 190°C. Thread marinated lamb pieces onto the soaked wooden skewers.
4. Cook lamb pinchos in your cooking basket within 5 mins on one side, carefully flip them over using tongs, then cook within 5 mins till cooked through.
5. Serve immediately with a choice of sides like couscous or fresh salad.

Nutritional Values: Calories: 441; Carbs: 3g; Fat: 32g; Protein: 31g

Welsh Glazed Honey-Lamb Lollipops

Preparation time: 15 minutes
Cooking time: 10-12 minutes
Servings: 4

Ingredients:
- Eight lamb lollipops (French-trimmed lamb chops)
- Two tbsp runny honey
- Two tbsp Worcestershire sauce
- Four garlic cloves, minced
- Two tsp fresh rosemary, chopped
- Salt & ground black pepper, as required
- Olive oil, for drizzling

Directions:
1. In your small container, whisk honey, Worcestershire sauce, minced garlic plus chopped rosemary to create the glaze.
2. Pat lamb lollipops dry using kitchen towel, then flavour with salt plus black pepper.
3. Drizzle some olive oil on each side of lamb lollipops, then rub the glaze onto each side, ensuring they are well coated.

4. Warm up your air fryer to 200°C. Put glazed lamb lollipops in your cooking basket.
5. Cook within 5-6 mins on each side till it reaches your desired level of doneness (62°C/145°F for medium-rare; 68°C/155°F for medium).

Nutritional Values: Calories: 420; Carbs: 16g; Fat: 28g; Protein: 26g

Parmesan and Herb-Crumbed Racks

Preparation time: 10 minutes
Cooking time: 20-30 minutes
Servings: 4

Ingredients:
- Two lamb racks (8 cutlets each), trimmed
- 100g freshly grated Parmesan cheese
- 75g breadcrumbs
- Two tbsp fresh parsley, chopped
- One tbsp fresh rosemary, chopped
- One tsp garlic powder
- Salt & ground black pepper, as required
- Olive oil, for drizzling

Directions:
1. In your shallow container, mix grated Parmesan cheese, breadcrumbs, parsley, rosemary, garlic powder, salt plus pepper.
2. Lay lamb racks on your cutting board with meat side facing up. Drizzle with olive oil on both sides and gently press the breadcrumb mixture onto the meat to create an even layer.
3. Warm up your air fryer to 180°C.
4. Place crusted lamb racks into your cooking basket. Cook within 20 mins for medium-rare or 30 mins for medium-well. Cool it down, carve, then serve.

Nutritional Values: Calories: 550; Carbs: 20g; Fat: 37g; Protein: 41g

Swiss Alpine Wine-Braised Shanks

Preparation time: 15 minutes
Cooking time: 50 minutes
Servings: 4

Ingredients:
- Four lamb shanks, approximately 1.5 kg in total
- Two tbsp vegetable oil
- One big onion, chopped
- Two carrots, chopped
- Two celery stalks, chopped
- Three garlic cloves, minced
- 500 ml Swiss alpine wine (such as Fendant or Chasselas)
- 500 ml beef stock
- Two sprigs each of rosemary & thyme
- Salt & ground black pepper, as required

Directions:
1. Warm up your air fryer to 180°C. Flavour lamb shanks using salt plus pepper on all sides.
2. In your big pan on moderate temp, add vegetable oil, then brown lamb shanks on all sides. Put aside.
3. In your same pan, add chopped onion, carrots, celery, plus minced garlic. Cook till vegetables are softened.
4. Add Swiss alpine wine to deglaze your pan, scraping up any browned bits. Allow the mixture to simmer and reduce by half.

5. Transfer the cooked vegetables and reduced wine sauce into a large baking dish or oven-safe dish that can fit inside your air fryer.
6. Place the browned lamb shanks on top of the vegetables in the prepared dish. Pour over the beef stock, then add rosemary and thyme sprigs.
7. Cover with aluminium foil and carefully put dish into your air fryer.
8. Cook within 20 mins at 180°C, adjust to 160°C, then cook within 20 mins till lamb shanks are tender. Serve.

Nutritional Values: Calories: 730; Carbs: 14g; Fat: 37g; Protein: 64g

FISH AND SEAFOOD

Crispy Fish and Chips

Preparation time: 20 minutes
Cooking time: 30 minutes
Servings: 4

Ingredients:
- Four white fish fillets (such as cod or haddock), about 200g each
- 100g plain flour
- Salt & pepper, as required
- Two big eggs, beaten
- 200g panko breadcrumbs
- Four big potatoes, washed & sliced into chips
- Cooking spray or olive oil

Directions:
1. Warm up your air fryer to 200°C.
2. Pat fish dry using kitchen paper, then flavour both sides with salt plus pepper.
3. Prepare three shallow dishes on your work surface: one with the flour, one with the beaten eggs, and one with the panko breadcrumbs.
4. Dredge each fish fillet in the flour, making sure it's evenly coated but shaking off any excess.
5. Dip the fillet into the beaten egg next, followed by the panko breadcrumbs, ensuring an even coating each time. Put aside.
6. In your container, toss chips, olive oil, salt plus pepper.
7. Put half of chips in your cooking basket. Air fry within 15 mins till golden brown, shaking once.
8. Take out the cooked chips and keep them warm while you cook the remaining batch of chips.
9. Once all chips are cooked, put breaded fish fillets in your cooking basket. Cook within 12-15 mins at 200°C till golden brown, flipping once.
10. Serve hot fish alongside tasty chips with tartare sauce or ketchup.

Nutritional Values: Calories: 715; Carbs: 77g; Fat: 22g; Protein: 45g

Lemon and Herb Cod Fillet

Preparation time: 10 minutes + marinating time
Cooking time: 12 minutes
Servings: 2

Ingredients:
- Two cod fillets (about 150g each)
- Zest & juice of one lemon
- Two tbsp chopped fresh parsley
- One tsp chopped fresh thyme
- One tsp chopped fresh rosemary
- Two garlic cloves, minced
- Three tbsp olive oil
- Salt & ground black pepper, as required

Directions:
1. In your small container, mix lemon zest, juice, parsley, thyme, rosemary, garlic, olive oil, salt plus black pepper. Put aside.

2. Pat dry cod fillets using kitchen paper. Put them in your shallow container. Pour marinade, then mix well. Cover, then marinate in your fridge within 30 mins.
3. Warm up your air fryer to 180°C. Remove marinated cod, then let it rest within 5 mins.
4. Carefully place each cod fillet in your cooking basket. Be sure not to overcrowd your air fryer.
5. Cook within 10-12 mins till fish flakes easily. Serve.

Nutritional Values: Calories: 354; Carbs: 3g; Fat: 23g; Protein: 34g

Spicy Cajun Prawns

Preparation time: 15 minutes
Cooking time: 12 minutes
Servings: 2

Ingredients:
- 400g raw king prawns, peeled & deveined
- One tbsp olive oil
- Two tbsp Cajun seasoning
- Juice of half a lemon
- Salt & pepper, as required

Directions:
1. In your big container, mix peeled king prawns with olive oil, Cajun seasoning, lemon juice, salt plus pepper, ensuring prawns are well coated. Marinate in your fridge within 10 mins.
2. Warm up your air fryer to 180°C. Put marinated prawns in your cooking basket.
3. Cook within 6 minutes on each side till prawns are cooked through and have an appealing golden brown.
4. Transfer cooked prawns to a serving dish and garnish with fresh coriander before serving.

Nutritional Values: Calories: 318; Carbs: 5g; Fat: 11g; Protein: 47g

Crispy Air-Fried Calamari

Preparation time: 15 minutes
Cooking time: 10 minutes
Servings: 4

Ingredients:
- 500g fresh squid, cleaned & sliced into rings
- 200g plain flour
- Two big eggs, beaten
- 200g panko breadcrumbs
- Salt & pepper, as required
- Olive oil spray
- Lemon wedges and tartare sauce for serving

Directions:
1. Clean and slice the squid into rings. Pat them dry with a kitchen towel and set aside.
2. Prepare three shallow plates or bowls. Place the flour on the first plate, the beaten eggs in the second bowl, and the panko breadcrumbs on the third plate. Season each with salt and pepper.
3. Dredge each squid ring first in flour, then beaten egg, and finally coat with panko breadcrumbs, pressing gently to ensure an even coating.
4. Warm up your air fryer to 190°C. Put breaded calamari rings in your cooking basket, ensuring not to overcrowd or overlap them.
5. Lightly spray the calamari with olive oil spray before cooking.

6. Cook within 10 mins till golden brown. Serve immediately with lemon wedges and tartare sauce for dipping.

Nutritional Values: Calories: 455; Carbs: 60g; Fat: 12g; Protein: 25g

Polish Breaded Perch Fillets

Preparation time: 15 minutes
Cooking time: 12 minutes
Servings: 4

Ingredients:
- Four perch fillets (150g each), pat dried
- 150g panko breadcrumbs
- 60g plain flour
- Two big eggs, beaten
- One tsp each paprika & garlic powder
- Salt & pepper, as required
- Olive oil spray

Directions:
1. Warm up your air fryer to 200°C. Flavour perch fillets with salt plus pepper.
2. In your shallow container, mix panko breadcrumbs, paprika, plus garlic powder.
3. Put flour in another shallow container, and beaten eggs in your third container.
4. Coat each perch fillet in flour, dip into beaten eggs, and press into breadcrumb mixture until evenly coated on both sides.
5. Put breaded fillets in your cooking basket. Lightly spray fillets with olive oil spray.
6. Cook within 10-12 mins till golden brown, flipping once. Serve.

Nutritional Values: Calories: 385; Carbs: 36g; Fat: 10g; Protein: 39g

Czech Fried Carp Fingers

Preparation time: 15 minutes
Cooking time: 12 minutes
Servings: 4

Ingredients:
- 500g carp fillets, cut into finger-sized strips
- 100g plain flour
- One tsp paprika
- Half tsp salt
- One-fourth tsp black pepper
- Two big eggs, beaten
- 150g panko breadcrumbs
- Cooking spray

Directions:
1. Warm up your air fryer to 200°C.
2. In your shallow plate, mix plain flour, paprika, salt, and black pepper.
3. Put beaten eggs in your container. Pour the panko breadcrumbs onto your separate plate.
4. Take each carp strip and coat it first in seasoned flour mixture, then dip it into beaten egg, ensuring it's fully coated. Finally, roll it in the panko breadcrumbs to cover the fish evenly. Set aside on a plate to prepare for frying.
5. Place the breaded carp fingers into your cooking basket. Lightly spray the fish with cooking spray.
6. Cook within 12 mins till golden brown. Halfway through cooking, ensure you flip the carp fingers to have an even cook on both sides. Serve.

Nutritional Values: Calories: 345; Carbs: 34g; Fat: 10g; Protein: 26g

Greek-Style Air Fryer Sea Bass

Preparation time: 15 minutes
Cooking time: 12 minutes
Servings: 4

Ingredients:

- Four sea bass fillets (approximately 200g each)
- Three tbsp olive oil
- Three garlic cloves, minced
- Juice of one lemon
- Zest of half a lemon
- One tsp dried oregano
- Salt & pepper, as required
- Two tbsp fresh parsley, chopped
- Approx. 40g pitted Kalamata olives, halved

Directions:

1. In your small container, mix olive oil, minced garlic, lemon juice, zest, dried oregano, salt, plus pepper.
2. Place the sea bass fillets in your shallow container, then pour marinade over them. Ensure all fillets are evenly coated with the marinade. Put aside.
3. Warm up your air fryer to 180°C. Put marinated sea bass fillets in your cooking basket. Cook within 10-12 mins till fish flakes easily.
4. In your small container, mix chopped parsley and halved olives.
5. Once cooked, remove the sea bass fillets from the air fryer and plate them individually.
6. Top each fillet with parsley and olive mixture. Serve.

Nutritional Values: Calories: 340; Carbs: 2g; Fat: 21g; Protein: 34g

Tuscan Lemon Sole

Preparation time: 15 minutes + marinating time
Cooking time: 15 minutes
Servings: 4
Ingredients:

- Four sole fillets, about 150g each
- 150ml dry white wine
- Zest and juice of one lemon
- Two garlic cloves, minced
- Two tbsp extra virgin olive oil
- One tsp dried Italian herbs (e.g. rosemary, thyme, oregano)
- Salt & ground black pepper, as required
- 100g cherry tomatoes, halved
- 20g capers, rinsed and drained

Directions:

1. In your shallow container, mix wine, lemon zest, juice, garlic, olive oil, plus Italian herbs.
2. Season the sole fillets with salt plus pepper, then put them in marinade. Refrigerate within 30 mins. Warm up your air fryer to 180°C.
3. Remove marinated sole fillets, then gently shake off excess liquid. Reserve the marinade.
4. Put marinated sole fillets in your cooking basket. Cook within 7-10 mins till cooked through and flaky, flipping once.
5. While the fish is cooking, pour the reserved marinade into a small saucepan along with cherry tomatoes and capers. Let it simmer on moderate temp till slightly thickened.

6. To serve, place each cooked sole fillet on individual plates and spoon over some pan sauce with cherry tomatoes and capers.

Nutritional Values: Calories: 354; Carbs: 6g; Fat: 12g; Protein: 42g

Garlic Butter Scallops

Preparation time: 10 minutes
Cooking time: 6 minutes
Servings: 4

Ingredients:

- 450g scallops, cleaned and patted dry
- Three cloves garlic, minced
- 60g unsalted butter, melted
- 30ml lemon juice
- Salt & ground black pepper, as required

Directions:

1. In your container, mix melted butter, minced garlic, lemon juice, salt, plus black pepper. Add scallops, giving them a good coating of the garlic butter mixture.
2. Warm up your air fryer to 200°C.
3. Put scallops in your cooking basket. Ensure that they are not overlapping to allow for even cooking.
4. Cook the scallops at 200°C for 6 minutes or until they are opaque and cooked through.
5. Once cooked, move scallops on your serving plate. Drizzle any remaining garlic butter from the air fryer basket over the scallops and garnish with chopped parsley.

Nutritional Values: Calories: 210; Carbs: 3g; Fat: 13g; Protein: 21g

Italian Zesty Mussels

Preparation time: 15 minutes
Cooking time: 10 minutes
Servings: 4

Ingredients:

- One kg fresh mussels, cleaned & debearded
- Two tbsp olive oil
- One small onion, finely chopped
- Two garlic cloves, minced
- 200ml white wine
- 400g tin chopped tomatoes
- One tsp each dried oregano & basil
- Salt & black pepper, as required

Directions:

1. Warm up your air fryer to 200°C.
2. In your big container, mix olive oil, onion, garlic, white wine, chopped tomatoes, oregano, basil, salt plus black pepper.
3. Add cleaned mussels, then toss until well-coated in the sauce. Transfer the mussels and sauce mixture into an air-fryer-safe dish.
4. Put dish in your cooking basket, then cook within 10 mins at 200°C, shaking basket once. Serve.

Nutritional Values: Calories: 260; Carbs: 12g; Fat: 11g; Protein: 21g

Parmesan-Crusted Haddock

Preparation time: 10 minutes
Cooking time: 12 minutes
Servings: 4

Ingredients:

- Four haddock fillets (about 150g each), pat dried
- 150g grated Parmesan cheese
- 75g breadcrumbs
- Two tsp dried parsley
- Half tsp garlic powder
- One-fourth tsp each ground black pepper & salt
- Two big eggs

Directions:

1. Pat the haddock fillets dry with paper towels.
2. In your medium shallow container, mix grated Parmesan cheese, breadcrumbs, dried parsley, garlic powder, salt plus black pepper.
3. In your separate shallow container, whisk two eggs. Dip each haddock fillet into the whisked eggs, ensuring they are fully coated.
4. Next, dip the egg-coated fillets into the breadcrumb mixture and press gently to adhere to both sides.
5. Spray your cooking basket using cooking spray. Put coated haddock fillets in your cooking basket with some space between each one.
6. Cook within 12 mins till golden brown, flipping once.

Nutritional Values: Calories: 389; Carbs: 18g; Fat: 17g; Protein: 38g

Spanish Clams and Chorizo

Preparation time: 10 minutes
Cooking time: 18 minutes
Servings: 4

Ingredients:

- 1.5 kg fresh clams, cleaned
- 225g Spanish chorizo, sliced
- Two tbsp olive oil
- One big onion, chopped
- Three garlic cloves, minced
- 400g can of diced tomatoes
- 250ml white wine (dry)
- Salt & ground black pepper, as required

Directions:

1. Warm up your air fryer to 200°C.
2. In your big container, toss clams in a little of the olive oil, then put aside.
3. Put chorizo slices in your cooking basket, then cook within 8 mins till crispy. Put aside.
4. In your big pan on moderate temp, add remaining olive oil, then sauté onion within 5 mins till softened. Add garlic, then cook within one min.
5. Pour canned tomatoes, white wine, cooked chorizo slices, salt plus pepper. Simmer within five mins.
6. Place clams into the tomato sauce mixture in your pan.
7. Carefully transfer clams with sauce to an air fryer-safe accessory (such as a shallow baking dish). Ensure it fits your air fryer dimensions ahead of time.
8. Cook in your air fryer at 200°C within 5 mins till all clams have opened and are cooked through. Discard any unopened clams.

Nutritional Values: Calories: 528; Carbs: 22g; Fat: 30g; Protein: 37g

British Whitebait Fry-up

Preparation time: 15 minutes
Cooking time: 8 minutes
Servings: 4

Ingredients:

- 450g fresh whitebait, cleaned
- 85g plain flour
- One tsp salt

- Half tsp black pepper
- One tbsp vegetable oil
- Lemon wedges & Tartare sauce, for serving

Directions:
1. Warm up your air fryer to 200°C.
2. In your big container, mix plain flour, salt, plus black pepper.
3. Ensure the whitebait are dry by patting them with kitchen paper. Then coat each fish in the flour mixture, making sure they are evenly covered.
4. Lightly spray or brush the air fryer basket with vegetable oil to prevent sticking.
5. Lay the floured whitebait in your cooking basket, taking care not to overcrowd them.
6. Cook within 4 mins before carefully flipping the whitebait using tongs or a spatula, then cook within 4 mins till golden brown.
7. Serve immediately with lemon wedges plus tartare sauce.

Nutritional Values: Calories: 262; Carbs: 16g; Fat: 12g; Protein: 24g

French Tuna Provençal

Preparation time: 15 minutes
Cooking time: 10 minutes
Servings: 4

Ingredients:
- Two tins of tuna in oil (about 200g each), drained
- One courgette, thinly sliced
- One each yellow & red pepper, deseeded & thinly sliced
- One big red onion, thinly sliced
- Two garlic cloves, minced
- Eight cherry tomatoes, halved
- 50g pitted black olives, halved
- Two tsp dried mixed herbs (such as basil, rosemary, thyme)
- Salt & ground black pepper, as required
- A drizzle of olive oil

Directions:
1. In your big container, mix drained tuna, courgette slices, red & yellow pepper slices, red onion slices, minced garlic, halved cherry tomatoes plus halved black olives.
2. Sprinkle over the mixed herbs, then flavour with salt plus black pepper. Drizzle some olive oil, then toss well.
3. Warm up your air fryer to 180°C.
4. Transfer the tuna mixture to your cooking basket. Cook within 10 mins at 180°C till vegetables are tender.
5. Serve your French Tuna Provençal hot with a side of crusty bread or over a bed of rice or pasta if desired.

Nutritional Values: Calories: 210; Carbs: 12g; Fat: 8g; Protein: 24g

Hungarian Catfish Paprikash

Preparation time: 15 minutes
Cooking time: 30 minutes
Servings: 4

Ingredients:
- 600g catfish fillets, cut into chunks
- Two tbsp olive oil
- One big onion, chopped finely
- Two garlic cloves, minced
- One red bell pepper, diced
- 400g canned chopped tomatoes

- One tbsp each paprika & sweet smoked paprika
- salt & black pepper, as required
- 250ml sour cream

Directions:
1. Warm up your air fryer to 200°C.
2. In your container, toss catfish chunks with olive oil. Put aside.
3. In your big pan, sauté onion and garlic on moderate temp till softened. Put bell pepper, then cook within 5 mins.
4. Stir in chopped tomatoes, both types of paprika, salt plus black pepper. Cook within 5 mins till five mixture thickens.
5. Gently fold in catfish pieces into the tomato mixture to coat them evenly.
6. Place the coated catfish chunks in the air fryer basket in a single layer to ensure even cooking.
7. Cook for about 10 minutes flipping halfway through or until fish is cooked thoroughly and flakes easily with a fork.
8. While the catfish is cooking, prepare sauce by mixing sour cream with some of the chopped dill in a bowl.
9. Once the catfish is cooked, serve hot on a plate with sauce on the side or drizzled over top of the Catfish Paprikash.

Nutritional Values: Calories: 470; Carbs: 14g; Fat: 27g; Protein: 41g

Portuguese Sardines & Peppers

Preparation time: 15 minutes
Cooking time: 10 minutes
Servings: 4

Ingredients:
- Eight fresh sardines, cleaned and gutted
- Two each yellow & red bell peppers, sliced into thin strips
- Three tbsp olive oil
- One tbsp smoked paprika
- Salt & black pepper, as required
- Juice of one lemon

Directions:
1. Warm up your air fryer to 190°C.
2. In your big container, mix sliced bell peppers, 2 tbsp olive oil, salt plus pepper.
3. Put bell pepper slices in your cooking basket, then cook within 5 mins.
4. Meanwhile, pat dry the sardines and rub them using remaining olive oil. Flavour with smoked paprika, salt, plus black pepper.
5. Remove basket, then arrange sardines on top. Cook within 5 mins till golden.
6. Squeeze lemon juice over the cooked sardines and bell peppers. Serve.

Nutritional Values: Calories: 349; Carbs: 6g; Fat: 25g; Protein: 26g

Norwegian Salmon Kebabs

Preparation time: 15 minutes
Cooking time: 10 minutes
Servings: 4

Ingredients:
- 600g Norwegian salmon fillet, skinless and cut into 2.5cm cubes
- Two red onions, chopped into quarters
- Two each yellow & red bell peppers, deseeded and chopped into 2.5cm squares
- One courgette, sliced into rounds
- Olive oil spray

- Salt & black pepper, as required

Directions:
1. Warm up your air fryer to 200°C.
2. Thread salmon cubes, red onion quarters, red and yellow bell pepper squares, and courgette rounds onto pre-soaked wooden skewers, alternating them as you go.
3. Lightly spray the assembled kebabs with olive oil spray, then flavour with salt plus black pepper. Arrange kebabs in your cooking basket.
4. Cook at 200°C within 10 mins till vegetables are tender. Carefully turn the kebabs halfway through cooking time to ensure even cooking. Serve.

Nutritional Values: Calories: 327; Carbs: 12g; Fat: 18g; Protein: 30g

Russian Zander Fishcakes

Preparation time: 15 minutes
Cooking time: 20 minutes
Servings: 4

Ingredients:
- 500g zander fillets, skin removed
- One big egg, beaten
- 100g wholewheat breadcrumbs
- Two tsp Dijon mustard
- One tbsp fresh chopped dill
- Salt & pepper, as required
- Olive oil spray, for cooking

Directions:
1. In your food processor, pulse zander fillets till finely minced. Transfer to your container.
2. Add beaten egg, breadcrumbs, Dijon mustard, chopped dill, salt plus pepper. Mix well.
3. With damp hands, divide it into 8, then shape each into a fishcake. Warm up your air fryer at 180°C.
4. Lightly spray fishcakes with olive oil spray on both sides and arrange them in your cooking basket.
5. Cook the fishcakes at 180°C for 10 mins. Flip each cake carefully using a spatula and cook for an additional 10 mins till golden brown. Serve.

Nutritional Values: Calories: 320; Carbs: 21g; Fat: 13g; Protein: 29g

German Beer-Battered Tilapia

Preparation time: 15 minutes
Cooking time: 10 minutes
Servings: 4

Ingredients:
- Four tilapia fillets (approx. 570 grams)
- 120 grams plain flour
- 180 ml German beer (lager or pilsner)
- One tsp each baking powder & paprika
- Salt & ground black pepper, as required
- Olive oil spray

Directions:
1. Pat tilapia fillets dry using paper towel, then flavour with salt plus ground black pepper. Put aside.
2. In your medium container, mix plain flour, baking powder, paprika, salt plus black pepper.

3. Slowly pour German beer while whisking the mixture until smooth. Warm up your air fryer to 200°C.
4. Dip each tilapia fillet into the beer batter to coat evenly, allowing any excess batter to drip off.
5. Place the battered tilapia fillets onto your cooking basket. Lightly spray the battered fillets with olive oil for a crispy finish.
6. Air-fry within 10 mins till golden brown, flipping once. Serve.

Nutritional Values: Calories: 322; Carbs: 23g; Fat: 7g; Protein: 38g

Austrian Creamy Marinated Lobster

Preparation time: 15 minutes
Cooking time: 30 minutes
Servings: 4

Ingredients:
- Four fresh lobster tails (approximately 140g each)
- 240ml white wine
- 60ml white wine vinegar
- One small onion, finely chopped
- Two garlic cloves, minced
- Two bay leaves
- One tbsp fresh thyme, chopped
- Salt & pepper, as required

For the Cream Sauce:
- 240ml double cream
- Fresh parsley, chopped for garnish

Directions:
1. In your big container, mix white wine, vinegar, onion, garlic, bay leaves, thyme, salt plus pepper. Add lobster tails, then refrigerate within one hour.
2. Warm up your air fryer to 180°C. Remove lobster tails from marinade, put aside, then reserve marinade.
3. Place lobster tails in your cooking basket, then cook within 12 -15 mins till fully cooked.
4. Meanwhile cook, pour reserved marinade into your saucepan, then boil on moderate temp. Adjust to low temp, then simmer within 10 mins to reduce by half.
5. Gradually whisk in the double cream until incorporated and smooth. Simmer within 5 mins on low temp till slightly thickened.
6. Once lobster tails are cooked, arrange them on serving plates. Pour a generous amount of creamy sauce over each lobster tail and garnish with parsley.

Nutritional Values: Calories: 443; Carbs: 8g; Fat: 27g; Protein: 36g

Zesty Oyster Fritters

Preparation time: 15 minutes
Cooking time: 10 minutes
Servings: 4

Ingredients:
- 250g fresh oysters, shucked and drained
- 125g plain flour
- One tsp baking powder
- Half tsp sea salt
- One-fourth tsp black pepper
- One big egg, lightly beaten
- 75ml whole milk
- One tbsp rapeseed oil
- Zest of one lemon
- Two spring onions, finely chopped
- Cooking spray for air fryer

Directions:

1. In your medium container, mix plain flour, baking powder, sea salt, plus black pepper.
2. In another container, mix beaten egg, whole milk, rapeseed oil, lemon zest, plus chopped spring onions. Combine it with dry mixture.
3. Gently fold in the drained oysters into the batter. Warm up your air fryer to 190°C. Lightly coat your basket using cooking spray.
4. Scoop tablespoon-sized dollops of batter onto the prepared air fryer basket, making sure not to overcrowd them.
5. Air fry within 10 mins till golden brown, flipping once. Serve.

Nutritional Values: Calories: 325; Carbs: 30g; Fat: 13g; Protein: 18g

VEGETABLE AND SIDES RECIPES

Garlic Parmesan Brussel Sprouts

Preparation time: 10 minutes
Cooking time: 15 minutes
Servings: 4

Ingredients:
- 450g Brussel sprouts, trimmed and halved
- Two tbsp olive oil
- Three garlic cloves, minced
- One tsp sea salt
- Half tsp ground black pepper
- 40g grated Parmesan cheese

Directions:
1. Warm up your air fryer to 180°C.
2. In your big container, mix Brussel sprouts, olive oil, minced garlic, sea salt, plus black pepper.
3. Put Brussel sprouts in your cooking basket.
4. Air fry the sprouts at 180°C within 15 mins till tender. Make sure to shake the basket halfway through cooking to promote even cooking.
5. Remove Brussel sprouts, then transfer them in your container. Add grated Parmesan cheese and toss gently until well combined. Serve.

Nutritional Values: Calories: 190; Carbs: 15g; Fat: 12g; Protein: 9g

Crispy Air-Fried Potatoes

Preparation time: 10 minutes
Cooking time: 20 minutes
Servings: 4

Ingredients:
- 800g baby potatoes, halved
- One tbsp olive oil
- One tsp each garlic & onion powder
- Half tsp smoked paprika
- Salt & pepper, as required

Directions:
1. In your big container, mix baby potatoes, olive oil, garlic powder, onion powder, smoked paprika, salt plus pepper.
2. Warm up your air fryer to 200°C. Carefully put seasoned potatoes into your cooking basket.
3. Air-fry the potatoes within 10 mins. Then, shake basket or use a spatula to turn the potatoes for even cooking.
4. Continue air-frying within 10 mins till crispy. Serve.

Nutritional Values: Calories: 212; Carbs: 34g; Fat: 6g; Protein: 4g

Italian Seasoned Asparagus

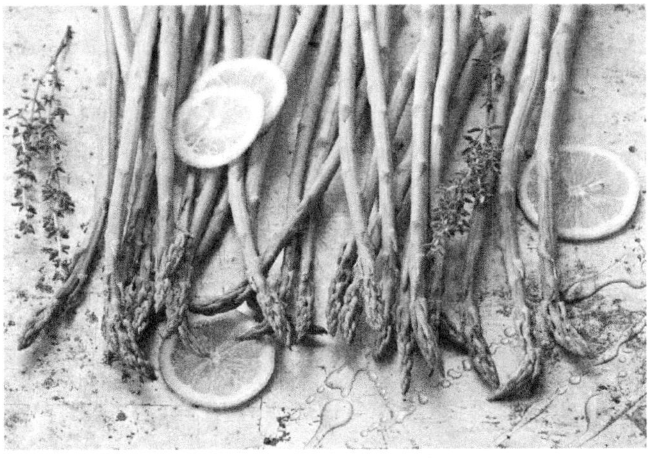

Preparation time: 5 minutes
Cooking time: 8-10 minutes
Servings: 4

Ingredients:
- 500g fresh asparagus, trimmed
- Two tbsp olive oil
- One tsp each onion & garlic powder
- One tbsp Italian seasoning
- Half tsp salt
- One-fourth tsp black pepper

Directions:
1. In your big container, mix olive oil, garlic powder, onion powder, Italian seasoning, salt, plus black pepper.
2. Put trimmed asparagus, then toss until evenly coated. Warm up your air fryer to 180°C.
3. Put seasoned asparagus in your cooking basket. Cook the asparagus within 8-10 mins till tender, shaking once. Serve.

Nutritional Values: Calories: 101; Carbs: 6g; Fat: 7g; Protein: 3g

Cheddar-Stuffed Mushrooms

Preparation time: 10 minutes
Cooking time: 8 minutes
Servings: 4

Ingredients:
- Twelve big closed cup mushrooms (approximately 225g)
- 100g mature cheddar cheese, grated
- 75g cream cheese
- One small onion, finely chopped
- Two garlic cloves, minced
- 50g breadcrumbs
- One tbsp chopped fresh parsley
- Salt & pepper, as required
- Olive oil spray

Directions:
1. Warm up your air fryer to 200°C.
2. Clean the mushrooms with a damp kitchen towel and remove the stems. Put aside.
3. In your container, mix grated cheddar cheese, cream cheese, chopped onion, minced garlic, breadcrumbs, plus chopped parsley. Flavour with salt plus pepper.
4. Stuff each mushroom cap with cheese mixture. Lightly spray your cooking basket using olive oil spray.
5. Put stuffed mushrooms into your cooking basket. Cook within 8 mins till mushrooms are tender. Serve.

Nutritional Values: Calories: 312; Carbs: 17g; Fat: 22g; Protein: 14g

Mediterranean Zucchini Fries

Preparation time: 15 minutes
Cooking time: 10 minutes
Servings: 4

Ingredients:
- Two big zucchinis, sliced into thick fries
- 50g plain flour
- Half tsp salt
- One-fourth tsp each black pepper & paprika
- One big egg, lightly beaten
- 100g panko breadcrumbs
- 25g grated Parmesan cheese
- Half tbsp dried mixed herbs (such as basil, oregano, and rosemary)
- Olive oil spray

Directions:
1. Warm up your air fryer to 180°C.
2. In your shallow container, mix flour, salt, pepper, plus paprika. In another shallow container, beat egg.
3. In your third shallow container, combine panko breadcrumbs, Parmesan cheese, and mixed herbs.
4. Dip each zucchini fry in flour mixture, beaten egg, then coat using breadcrumb mixture. Ensure each fry is evenly coated with each layer.
5. Place the prepared zucchini fries in your cooking basket. Lightly oil using olive oil cooking spray.
6. Cook within 10 mins at 180°C till fries are crisp, shaking basket once. Serve immediately with your favourite dipping sauce.

Nutritional Values: Calories: 250; Carbs: 34g; Fat: 8g; Protein: 12g

Cheesy Cauliflower Bites

Preparation time: 15 minutes
Cooking time: 12 minutes
Servings: 4

Ingredients:
- One medium cauliflower head (about 600g), sliced into florets
- 100g grated Cheddar cheese
- 75g panko breadcrumbs
- 50g grated Parmesan cheese
- One big egg, beaten
- Salt & black pepper, as required
- Cooking oil spray

Directions:
1. Warm up your air fryer to 190°C.
2. In your big container, mix Cheddar cheese, panko breadcrumbs, Parmesan cheese, salt plus pepper.
3. In your separate container, place beaten egg.
4. Dip each cauliflower floret in beaten egg, then coat with cheese mixture, pressing it onto the florets for better adherence.
5. Put coated cauliflower bites on your plate.
6. Lightly oil your cooking basket using cooking oil spray. Carefully put coated cauliflower bites in your cooking basket.
7. Cook within 12-15 mins till golden brown, flipping once. Serve.

Nutritional Values: Calories: 243; Carbs: 15g; Fat: 13g; Protein: 17g

Herbed Potato Wedges

Preparation time: 10 minutes
Cooking time: 20 minutes
Servings: 4

Ingredients:
- 800g potatoes, cut into wedges
- Two tbsp olive oil
- Two tsp mixed herbs (parsley, rosemary, and thyme)
- Half tsp garlic powder
- Salt & pepper, as required

Directions:
1. Warm up your air fryer to 200°C.
2. In your big container, toss potato wedges plus olive oil until evenly coated.

3. Add mixed herbs, garlic powder, salt, plus pepper, then toss again till wedges are well-seasoned.
4. Place the herbed potato wedges in your cooking basket, ensuring that they don't overlap.
5. Cook within 20 mins till crispy, shaking your basket once. Serve.

Nutritional Values: Calories: 260; Carbs: 40g; Fat: 8g; Protein: 5g

Greek-Style Green Beans

Preparation time: 10 minutes
Cooking time: 15 minutes
Servings: 4

Ingredients:

- 400g trimmed fresh green beans
- Two tbsp olive oil
- Two garlic cloves, minced
- 150g cherry tomatoes, halved
- One small red onion, thinly sliced
- 100g feta cheese, crumbled
- Two tsp dried oregano
- Salt & pepper, as required

Directions:
1. In your big container, mix green beans, olive oil, plus minced garlic. Toss well to coat the beans evenly.
2. Warm up your air fryer to 180°C.
3. Put seasoned green beans in your cooking basket. Cook within 10 mins, shaking your basket once.
4. Meanwhile, in your medium container, mix cherry tomatoes, red onion, feta cheese, plus dried oregano.
5. Add tomato-onion mixture to your cooking basket, then cook within 5 mins till vegetables are tender. Remove, then flavour with salt plus pepper. Serve.

Nutritional Values: Calories: 204; Carbs: 14g; Fat: 13g; Protein: 6g

Buttery Garlic Corn on the Cob

Preparation time: 5 minutes
Cooking time: 15 minutes
Servings: 4

Ingredients:

- Four corn on the cobs, husked & cleaned
- 60g unsalted butter, softened
- Five cloves of garlic, minced
- Salt & pepper, as required

Directions:
1. In your small container, mix softened butter, minced garlic, salt, plus pepper.
2. Spread the mixture evenly onto each corn cob, covering all sides of the cob. Warm up your air fryer to 180°C.
3. Put seasoned corn cobs into your cooking basket. Air-fry within 15 mins, rotating the cobs halfway through cooking time to ensure even cooking. Serve.

Nutritional Values: Calories: 235; Carbs: 29g; Fat: 13g; Protein: 4g

Pesto Tomato Snaps

Preparation time: 10 minutes
Cooking time: 8 minutes
Servings: 4

Ingredients:

- 200g cherry tomatoes
- 100g fresh basil leaves
- 50g pine nuts
- Two garlic cloves
- 60ml olive oil, extra-virgin
- 30g grated Parmesan cheese
- Salt & pepper, as required
- Eight slices wholemeal bread

Directions:

1. Warm up your air fryer to 180°C.
2. In your food processor, mix basil leaves, pine nuts, garlic, salt, plus pepper. Pulse till coarsely chopped.
3. Gradually add the olive oil while continuing to pulse, stopping to scrape down the sides as needed.
4. Mix in grated Parmesan cheese, then put aside. Cut the cherry tomatoes in half.
5. Arrange the bread slices on a cutting board and evenly spread each slice with the prepared pesto.
6. Place the halved tomatoes on top of each pesto-covered bread slice. Press gently to secure the tomatoes in place.
7. Transfer the pesto tomato snaps to your cooking basket. Air fry within 6-8 mins till bread is toasted. Serve.

Nutritional Values: Calories: 452; Carbs: 33g; Fat: 30g; Protein: 13g

Mozzarella-Baked Eggplant Roulades

Preparation time: 20 minutes
Cooking time: 20 minutes
Servings: 4

Ingredients:

- One big eggplant, thinly sliced lengthways (about 500g)
- Two tbsp olive oil
- 200g fresh mozzarella, thinly sliced
- 100g grated Parmesan cheese
- 100g baby spinach leaves
- Two tsp dried mixed herbs (such as basil, oregano, and thyme)
- Salt & pepper, as required

Directions:

1. Warm up your air fryer to 180°C.
2. Brush each eggplant slice using olive oil, then flavour with salt plus pepper.
3. Air-fry eggplant slices in your cooking basket within 5 mins each side till softened but still retaining the shape.
4. On each eggplant slice, place a layer of spinach leaves, followed by a slice of mozzarella and a generous sprinkle of grated Parmesan. Sprinkle dried mixed herbs over each piece.
5. Roll up each eggplant slice carefully to enclose the filling and secure with a toothpick if needed.
6. Place rolled eggplant roulades seam-side down back in your cooking basket. Cook within 10-12 mins at 180°C till golden brown.
7. Carefully remove roulades from the air fryer using tongs or a spatula, serve warm with your favourite dipping sauce or a side salad.

Nutritional Values: Calories: 395; Carbs: 10g; Fat: 30g; Protein: 24g

Creamy Spinach Artichoke Dip

Preparation time: 10 minutes
Cooking time: 20 minutes
Servings: 6

Ingredients:

- 150g fresh spinach, chopped
- One (400g) can artichoke hearts, drained and chopped
- 225g cream cheese, softened
- 60ml mayonnaise
- 60ml sour cream
- One small onion, finely chopped
- Two garlic cloves, minced
- 80g grated cheddar cheese
- 50g grated mozzarella cheese

- Salt & pepper, as required

Directions:
1. In your big container, mix chopped spinach, artichoke hearts, cream cheese, mayonnaise, sour cream, onion, plus garlic.
2. Add in the cheddar and mozzarella cheeses. Flavour with salt plus pepper, mixing till fully incorporated.
3. Transfer the dip into an air fryer-safe baking dish that fits comfortably inside your air fryer.
4. Warm up your air fryer to 180°C. Put baking dish on your cooking basket, then cook at 180°C within 20 mins till bubbling and golden brown on top. Serve.

Nutritional Values: Calories: 310; Carbs: 11g; Fat: 25g; Protein: 10g

Stuffed Bell Peppers with Quinoa

Preparation time: 15 minutes
Cooking time: 41 minutes
Servings: 4

Ingredients:
- Four big bell peppers, tops removed and seeds scooped out
- 150g uncooked quinoa
- 350ml vegetable broth
- One tbsp olive oil
- One onion, finely chopped
- Two cloves of garlic, minced
- 200g canned sweetcorn, drained
- 200g canned black beans, drained and rinsed
- 150g cherry tomatoes, halved
- 50g grated cheddar cheese
- Salt & pepper, as required

Directions:
1. Rinse the quinoa under cold water in a fine mesh strainer for about a minute.
2. In your saucepan on moderate temp, mix quinoa plus broth. Let it boil, adjust to low temp, cover, then cook within 15 mins till quinoa is cooked. Remove, then put aside.
3. Warm up your air fryer to 180°C.
4. In your frying pan on moderate temp, add olive oil. Add chopped onion, then cook within 5 mins till softened. Put minced garlic, then cook within 1-2 mins till fragrant.
5. In your big container, mix cooked quinoa, onion-garlic mixture, sweetcorn, black beans, cherry tomatoes plus 1/2 grated cheddar cheese. Flavour with salt plus pepper.
6. Fill each bell pepper using quinoa mixture until full. Put them standing up in your air fryer basket or drawer.
7. Cook within 15 mins at 180°C till bell peppers are tender. Top each pepper using rest of cheese, then cook within 5 mins till cheese is melted. Serve.

Nutritional Values: Calories: 346; Carbs: 53g; Fat: 9g; Protein: 15g

Ratatouille Vegetable Bake

Preparation time: 20 minutes
Cooking time: 25 minutes
Servings: 4

Ingredients:
- One big each aubergine & courgette, sliced into rounds
- Two medium red peppers, cut into strips
- One big red onion, chopped

- Four garlic cloves, minced
- 400g tin of chopped tomatoes
- Two tbsp olive oil
- One tsp dried basil
- Half tsp dried oregano
- Salt & pepper, as required

Directions:
1. In your big container, mix sliced courgette, aubergine, red pepper plus onion. Drizzle using olive oil, then flavour with salt plus pepper. Toss till vegetables are evenly coated in oil and seasoning.
2. Warm up your air fryer to 180°C.
3. Arrange half of the vegetables in your cooking basket. Remember not to overcrowd the basket. Cook within 15 mins, stirring once.
4. Carefully remove cooked vegetables into your big container. Do same step using rest of vegetables.
5. In your saucepan on moderate temp, mix minced garlic, tin of chopped tomatoes, dried basil plus oregano. Flavour with salt plus pepper. Simmer within 10 mins till sauce thickens slightly.
6. Pour over cooked vegetables in the dish, then toss well. Serve.

Nutritional Values: Calories: 180; Carbs: 22g; Fat: 9g; Protein: 4g

Rosemary Baby Carrots

Preparation time: 10 minutes
Cooking time: 20 minutes
Servings: 4

Ingredients:
- 450g baby carrots, washed and peeled
- Two tbsp olive oil
- Two tsp fresh chopped rosemary
- Half tsp sea salt
- One-fourth tsp black pepper, freshly ground

Directions:
1. In your big container, mix baby carrots, olive oil, rosemary, sea salt, plus black pepper.
2. Warm up your air fryer to 180°C. Put seasoned baby carrots in your cooking basket.
3. Cook baby carrots within 20 mins till tender, shaking your basket once. Serve.

Nutritional Values: Calories: 114; Carbs: 14g; Fat: 6g; Protein: 1g

Spanish Patatas Bravas

Preparation time: 15 minutes
Cooking time: 40 minutes
Servings: 4

Ingredients:
- 800g potatoes, peeled & sliced into small cubes
- One tbsp olive oil
- One & half tsp smoked paprika
- Half tsp garlic granules
- Salt & black pepper, as required

For the Bravas Sauce:
- Two tbsp olive oil
- One small onion, finely chopped
- Two garlic cloves, minced
- One (400g) can chopped tomatoes
- One tsp smoked paprika
- One-fourth tsp cayenne pepper
- Salt & black pepper, as required

Directions:
1. In your big container, toss potatoes, olive oil, smoked paprika, garlic granules, salt, plus black pepper. Warm up your air fryer to 200°C.

2. Put potato cubes in your cooking basket. Cook within 25 mins till crispy, shaking basket once.
3. While the potatoes are cooking, prepare the bravas sauce by heating the olive oil in your medium saucepan on moderate temp. Add onions plus garlic, sautéing till soft and translucent.
4. Put chopped tomatoes, smoked paprika, cayenne pepper, salt plus black pepper. Simmer within 15 mins till sauce thickens slightly.
5. Put cooked potatoes into your serving dish, then pour bravas sauce. Serve.

Nutritional Values: Calories: 348; Carbs: 52g; Fat: 12g; Protein: 9g

Swedish Hasselback Potatoes

Preparation time: 15 minutes
Cooking time: 45 minutes
Servings: 4

Ingredients:
- Eight medium potatoes (Maris Piper or King Edward)
- Two tbsp sunflower oil
- Salt & ground black pepper, as required
- Two tbsp melted butter
- Two garlic cloves, minced

Directions:
1. Rinse and thoroughly dry the potatoes. Slice each potato width wise at 3mm intervals.
2. In your small container, mix sunflower oil, sea salt, plus black pepper. Brush each potato with the oil mixture, ensuring it seeps into the slices.
3. Warm up your air fryer to 180°C. Put potatoes in your cooking basket, then cook within 30 mins.
4. Mix together the melted butter and minced garlic in a small bowl. Brush the potatoes with this mixture, ensuring it gets between the slices.
5. Continue to air fry within 15 mins till potatoes are golden brown. Serve.

Nutritional Values: Calories: 232; Carbs: 35g; Fat: 9g; Protein: 4g

Air Fryer Feta-Stuffed Olives

Preparation time: 15 minutes
Cooking time: 8 minutes
Servings: 6

Ingredients:
- 24 large green olives, pitted
- 100g feta cheese, crumbled
- One tsp fresh parsley, chopped
- Half tsp lemon zest
- ground black pepper, as required
- 50g plain flour
- One big egg, beaten
- 75g panko breadcrumbs

Directions:
1. In your small container, mix crumbled feta cheese, parsley, lemon zest plus black pepper. Put aside.
2. Use a small spoon or piping bag to fill each pitted olive with the feta mixture.
3. Prepare your coating station by placing flour in one shallow container, beaten egg in another and panko breadcrumbs in a third dish.

4. Roll each stuffed olive in flour, dip it in beaten egg, then coat it evenly in breadcrumbs.
5. War up your air fryer at 190°C. Gently place the coated olives in your cooking basket. Cook within 8 mins till golden brown, shaking your basket once. Serve.

Nutritional Values: Calories: 173; Carbs: 17g; Fat: 9g; Protein: 7g

Crunchy Beetroot Chips

Preparation time: 10 minutes
Cooking time: 20 minutes
Servings: 4

Ingredients:
- Four medium beetroots, thoroughly washed and peeled
- One tbsp olive oil
- One-fourth tsp each sea salt & black pepper

Directions:
1. Slice the beetroots thinly using a mandolin or sharp knife, ensuring that all slices are of uniform thickness.
2. In your big container, toss beetroot slices, olive oil, sea salt, plus black pepper.
3. Warm up your air fryer to 180°C. Arrange beetroot slices in your cooking basket, avoiding overlap.
4. Cook within 20 mins, tossing and shaking the basket halfway through cooking to ensure even crispiness. Serve.

Nutritional Values: Calories: 87; Carbs: 10g; Fat: 5g; Protein: 2g

Thyme-Roasted Parsnips

Preparation time: 10 minutes
Cooking time: 25 minutes
Servings: 4

Ingredients:
- 500g parsnips, peeled & sliced into evenly sized batons
- One tbsp olive oil
- Two tsp fresh thyme leaves, chopped
- Sea salt & ground black pepper, as required

Directions:
1. Warm up your air fryer to 180°C.
2. In your big container, mix parsnip batons, olive oil, thyme leaves, salt, plus pepper.
3. Arrange parsnips in your cooking basket, ensuring there is enough space between them for proper air circulation.
4. Cook within 25 mins till parsnips are golden, shaking the basket halfway through cooking to ensure even cooking. Serve.

Nutritional Values: Calories: 162; Carbs: 22g; Fat: 7g; Protein: 2g

Tuscan Onion Rings

Preparation time: 15 minutes
Cooking time: 8-10 minutes
Servings: 4

Ingredients:

- Two big onions, sliced into rings
- 150g plain flour
- One tsp salt
- Half tsp each black pepper, garlic powder, dried basil & dried oregano
- 250ml whole milk
- 100g Panko breadcrumbs
- Cooking spray

Directions:

1. In your shallow container, mix plain flour, salt, black pepper, garlic powder, dried basil, plus dried oregano.
2. Pour the whole milk into your separate shallow container. Put Panko breadcrumbs in your third shallow container.
3. Dip each onion ring first in flour mixture, in milk, then coat with breadcrumbs. Warm up your air fryer to 190°C.
4. Attach baking paper onto the air fryer basket and arrange the coated onion rings in a single layer (Work in batches if necessary).
5. Spray the onion rings with cooking spray to contribute to an even golden crisp. Cook within 8-10 mins till golden brown, tossing once. Serve.

Nutritional Values: Calories: 350; Carbs: 63g; Fat: 4g; Protein: 11g

SNACKS & APPETIZERS

Crispy Air Fryer Bruschetta

Preparation time: 10 minutes
Cooking time: 5 minutes
Servings: 6

Ingredients:
- One loaf of ciabatta bread (approx. 250g), cut into 1cm thick slices
- Three tbsp olive oil
- Two medium tomatoes, finely diced
- One small red onion, finely diced
- Two garlic cloves, minced
- 20g fresh basil leaves, chopped
- Salt & pepper, as required
- Balsamic vinegar, for drizzling

Directions:
1. Warm up your air fryer to 180°C.
2. Put ciabatta slices in your big container, then drizzle with olive oil. Toss well.
3. Transfer the oiled ciabatta slices to your cooking basket. Cook within 3-5 mins till golden brown.
4. Whilst the bread cools slightly, mix together the tomatoes, red onion, minced garlic and chopped basil in your small container. Flavour with salt plus pepper.
5. Top each toasted ciabatta slice with a generous spoonful of tomato mixture. Drizzle with balsamic vinegar. Serve.

Nutritional Values: Calories: 228; Carbs: 32g; Fat: 8g; Protein: 7g

Feta Cheese Rolls

Preparation time: 20 minutes
Cooking time: 15 minutes
Servings: 4 (12 rolls)

Ingredients:
- 200g feta cheese, crumbled
- 100g spinach, chopped
- Two spring onions, finely chopped
- One-fourth tsp nutmeg, ground
- Salt & pepper, as required
- 12 sheets of filo pastry, each cut into thirds lengthwise
- 50g melted butter or olive oil, to brush pastry

Directions:
1. In your medium container, mix crumbled feta cheese with chopped spinach, finely chopped spring onions, ground nutmeg, salt plus pepper. Put aside.
2. Lay out filo pastry strip on your clean work surface; brush lightly using melted butter or olive oil.
3. Place a heaped spoonful of the feta cheese mixture at the bottom end of the strip. Fold in both sides and roll it up into a snug parcel.

4. Repeat steps 2 and 3 until all the filling has been used, making approximately 12 feta cheese rolls.
5. Warm up your air fryer to 180°C. Lightly coat your cooking basket using non-stick spray.
6. Arrange feta cheese rolls in your cooking basket, leaving space between them for even cooking.
7. Cook within 15 mins at 180°C till golden, flipping once. Serve.

Nutritional Values: Calories: 432; Carbs: 37g; Fat: 24g; Protein: 14g

Cheesy Potato Bites

Preparation time: 15 minutes
Cooking time: 12-15 minutes
Servings: 4

Ingredients:
- 450g potatoes, peeled and grated
- 100g cheddar cheese, grated
- 50g breadcrumbs
- Half tsp each salt & garlic powder
- One-fourth tsp black pepper
- One big egg, beaten
- Cooking spray

Directions:
1. In your big container, mix grated potatoes, grated cheddar cheese, breadcrumbs, salt, black pepper, plus garlic powder. Add beaten egg, then mix well.
2. Warm up your air fryer to 200°C.
3. Shape the potato mixture into small balls, then arrange them on your plate or tray.
4. Lightly spray your cooking basket using cooking spray.
5. Put potato bites into your cooking basket, ensuring there's enough space between them for even cooking.
6. Cook within 12-15 mins till golden brown, turning them once. Serve.

Nutritional Values: Calories: 285; Carbs: 36g; Fat: 10g; Protein: 11g

French Ratatouille Skewers

Preparation time: 20 minutes
Cooking time: 10 minutes
Servings: 4

Ingredients:
- One each medium courgette & aubergine, cubed
- One each yellow & red pepper, deseeded & cubed
- 200g cherry tomatoes
- Two tbsp olive oil
- One tsp each dried basil & oregano
- Salt & pepper, as required

Directions:
1. In your big container, mix cubed aubergine, courgette, red and yellow peppers, and cherry tomatoes.
2. Add olive oil, dried basil, dried oregano, salt, plus pepper. Toss gently to coat all the vegetables evenly.
3. Warm up your air fryer to 200°C.
4. Thread vegetables onto your metal skewers, alternating between different types of vegetables. Be mindful not to overcrowd the skewers.

5. Place the ratatouille skewers in your cooking basket. Cook within 10 mins at 200°C, turning once till all sides are browned. Serve.
Nutritional Values: Calories: 143; Carbs: 18g; Fat: 8g; Protein: 3g

Italian Arancini Balls

Preparation time: 15 minutes
Cooking time: 20 minutes
Servings: 12 arancini balls

Ingredients:
- 200g cooked Arborio rice, cooled
- 75g grated mozzarella cheese
- 50g diced pepperoni
- 40g grated Parmesan cheese
- One big egg, beaten
- 70g plain flour
- 100g breadcrumbs
- Salt & black pepper, as required
- Olive oil spray

Directions:
1. In your big container, mix cooked Arborio rice, grated mozzarella, diced pepperoni, and grated Parmesan cheese. Flavour with salt plus black pepper.
2. Using dampened hands, shape it into 12 balls.
3. Roll each ball in the beaten egg, then coat with plain flour, making sure to shake off any excess flour. Next, roll each ball in breadcrumbs until evenly coated.
4. Warm up your air fryer to 200°C.
5. Put arancini balls into your cooking basket, leaving enough space between them for even cooking.
6. Lightly spray the balls with olive oil spray for a golden-brown finish. Cook the arancini balls within 20 mins till crispy, turning once. Serve.

Nutritional Values: Calories: 372; Carbs: 45g; Fat: 13g; Protein: 17g

Mediterranean Zucchini Fritters

Preparation time: 10 minutes
Cooking time: 20 minutes
Servings: 4

Ingredients:
- Two medium-sized zucchinis, coarsely grated
- 100g feta cheese, crumbled
- One small red onion, finely chopped
- One garlic clove, minced
- 80g plain flour
- One tsp baking powder
- Half tsp sea salt
- One-fourth tsp ground black pepper
- Two big eggs, lightly beaten
- Two tbsp each fresh mint & parsley, chopped
- Olive oil spray

Directions:
1. Put grated zucchini in your colander, then sprinkle with salt. Allow to sit for about 5 minutes, then squeeze out any excess water.
2. In your container, mix grated zucchini, crumbled feta cheese, red onion, garlic, flour, baking powder, sea salt plus black pepper.
3. Add beaten eggs, then mix well to create the fritter batter. Fold in the fresh parsley and mint leaves to add some Mediterranean flavour.

4. Warm up your air fryer to 200°C. Lightly oil your cooking basket using olive oil spray.
5. Using an ice cream scoop or tablespoon measure, drop dollops of fritter batter into your cooking basket.
6. Cook within 10 mins at 200°C before flipping, then cooking them for an additional 10 minutes till golden brown. Serve.

Nutritional Values: Calories: 210; Carbs: 23g; Fat: 9g; Protein: 10g

Spicy Spanish Chorizo Slices

Preparation time: 5 minutes
Cooking time: 15 minutes
Servings: 2

Ingredients:
- 200g Spanish chorizo sausage, sliced into 1cm thick slices
- One tbsp olive oil
- Half tsp smoked paprika
- One-fourth tsp cayenne pepper
- Salt & black pepper, as required

Directions:
1. In your medium container, mix chorizo slices, olive oil, smoked paprika, cayenne pepper, salt, plus black pepper. Mix well to coat the chorizo evenly with the spices.
2. Warm up your air fryer to 180°C. Place prepared chorizo slices in your cooking basket, ensuring they do not overlap.
3. Cook within 15 mins till crispy and golden brown, turning once. Serve.

Nutritional Values: Calories: 475; Carbs: 2g; Fat: 39g; Protein: 27g

Eggplant Parmesan Rounds

Preparation time: 15 minutes
Cooking time: 18 minutes
Servings: 4

Ingredients:
- One big aubergine, cut into 1 cm thick rounds
- 100 g plain flour
- Two big free-range eggs, beaten
- 200 g panko breadcrumbs
- 100 g grated Parmesan cheese
- Two tsp dried oregano
- Salt & pepper, as required
- Cooking spray

Directions:
1. Warm up your air fryer to 200°C.
2. In your shallow container, put plain flour. In another shallow container, place beaten eggs. In your third shallow container, mix panko breadcrumbs, grated Parmesan cheese plus dried oregano.
3. Season the cut aubergine slices with salt and pepper.
4. Coat each aubergine round in flour. Dip it into beaten egg. Finally, press it into the breadcrumb mixture to ensure an even coating on both sides.
5. Lightly spray the prepared aubergine rounds with cooking spray on both sides.
6. Carefully transfer the coated aubergine rounds into your cooking basket.
7. Cook within 9 mins at 200°C, then carefully turn over each round, then cook within 9 mins till crisp. Serve.

Nutritional Values: Calories: 415; Carbs: 58g; Fat: 12g; Protein: 20g

Russian Piroshki Puffs

Preparation time: 15 minutes + resting time
Cooking time: 20 minutes
Servings: 4

Ingredients:
- 250g plain flour
- One tsp instant yeast
- One tbsp granulated sugar
- 200ml warm water
- Two tbsp vegetable oil, plus extra for greasing the air fryer
- 300g minced beef or lamb
- One medium-sized onion, finely chopped (approx. 100g)
- One garlic clove, minced
- A handful of chopped fresh parsley (approx. 15g)
- Salt & black pepper, as required

Directions:
1. In your big container, mix flour, instant yeast, sugar, warm water, plus salt. Mix well till a dough forms.
2. Knead dough for about 5 minutes, then place it back in the bowl. Cover and let it rest within 1 hour.
3. In your pan within 1 tbsp oil on moderate temp, cook minced meat, breaking it up as it cooks.
4. Once browned, put onion plus garlic, then continue cooking till soft. Flavour with salt plus pepper. Remove, then stir in chopped fresh parsley.
5. Warm up your air fryer to 180°C. Brush some oil on the racks or use an oil spray.
6. Once the dough has doubled in size, divide it into eight. Roll each piece out into a circle about half a centimetre thick.
7. Put spoonful of filling in centre of each dough circle.
8. Fold the dough over, sealing the edges with a fork. If the dough doesn't stick, moisten the edges slightly with water.
9. Place the piroshki in your cooking basket. Air fry within 12-15 mins, turning once till golden brown. Serve.

Nutritional Values: Calories: 671; Carbs: 61g; Fat: 34g; Protein: 26g

Swedish Kanelbullar Rolls

Preparation time: 20 minutes + rising time
Cooking time: 12 minutes
Servings: 10 rolls

Ingredients:
- 300ml milk, warmed
- 7g active dry yeast
- 100g caster sugar
- 500g plain flour
- Half tsp salt
- One tsp ground cardamom
- 75g unsalted butter, dissolve & cooled
- One egg, beaten

For the Filling:
- 100g unsalted butter, softened
- 50g caster sugar
- Two tbsp cinnamon, ground

Glaze:
- Two tbsp golden syrup
- Water, as required

Directions:

1. In your big container, mix warmed milk, yeast plus sugar. Let it sit for about 5 minutes until frothy.
2. Add flour, salt, cardamom, cooled melted butter, and beaten egg. Mix till a smooth dough forms.
3. Cover using a damp cloth, then let it rise in a warm place within 1 hour till doubled in size.
4. Turn out dough onto your floured surface, then roll out into a large rectangle (about 30x40cm).
5. To prepare the filling, mix together softened butter, sugar, plus cinnamon in your small bowl. Spread filling evenly over rolled-out dough.
6. Roll up the dough tightly into a log shape starting from one long edge. Slice the log into ten equal pieces using a sharp knife or unflavoured dental floss.
7. Place parchment paper or grease your air fryer basket with some oil or butter to prevent sticking.
8. Place five slices evenly spaced in the air fryer basket; avoid overcrowding as they expand during cooking.
9. Cook within 12 mins at 180°C till golden brown. Use a toothpick to test the rolls; it should come out clean. Repeat with the remaining slices.
10. To make the glaze, mix golden syrup with a pinch of water. Brush the warm rolls with the glaze and let them cool slightly before serving.

Nutritional Values: Calories: 450; Carbs: 72g; Fat: 16g; Protein: 8g

German Pretzel Bites

Preparation time: 20 minutes
Cooking time: 8 minutes
Servings: 4

Ingredients:
- 450g plain flour
- One tsp salt
- One tbsp caster sugar
- One packet (7g) instant yeast
- 300ml warm water
- Two tbsp vegetable oil
- 60g bicarbonate of soda
- Two big eggs, beaten
- Coarse sea salt, for topping

Directions:
1. In your big container, mix plain flour, teaspoon of salt, caster sugar, plus instant yeast.
2. Mix in the warm water and vegetable oil until the dough comes together. Knead it on your floured surface till elastic.
3. Divide it into 24 equal pieces, then roll each into a small ball. Warm up your air fryer to 190°C.
4. In your shallow container, dissolve the bicarbonate of soda in 120ml of warm water.
5. Dip each dough ball into the bicarbonate solution and then quickly roll in the beaten eggs. Place the balls onto an air fryer's greased basket, making sure they are not touching each other.
6. Sprinkle each pretzel bite with coarse sea salt. Air fry within 8 mins till golden brown. Serve.

Nutritional Values: Calories: 628; Carbs: 68g; Fat: 14g; Protein: 17g

Bosnian Spinach and Cheese Pies

Preparation time: 30 minutes
Cooking time: 20 minutes
Servings: 6

Ingredients:

- 500g fresh spinach leaves, washed & chopped
- 250g feta cheese, crumbled
- 150g sour cream
- One big egg, beaten
- One tsp salt
- Half tsp black pepper
- 450g puff pastry, thawed
- Flour for dusting
- Olive oil for brushing

Directions:

1. In your big container, mix chopped spinach, crumbled feta cheese, sour cream, beaten egg, salt, plus pepper. Put aside.
2. Roll out puff pastry in your floured surface to 5mm thickness. Slice the dough into six equal squares.
3. Place a generous amount of the spinach and cheese mixture onto the centre of each pastry square.
4. Fold pastry corners over filling to form a triangular pie, sealing edges with a little water.
5. Warm up your air fryer to 180°C. Lightly grease each pie using olive oil on all sides.
6. Put pies in your cooking basket, then cook within 20 mins till golden brown. Serve.

Nutritional Values: Calories: 583; Carbs: 42g; Fat: 41g; Protein: 15g

Belgian Vol-au-Vent Pastries

Preparation time: 20 minutes
Cooking time: 25 minutes
Servings: 6

Ingredients:

- 320g ready-to-use puff pastry
- Six tbsp crème fraîche
- 150g mixed mushrooms, chopped
- One shallot, finely diced
- Two garlic cloves, minced
- 100g cooked ham, diced
- One sprig of fresh thyme, leaves only & chopped
- Salt & pepper, as required
- One beaten egg, for glazing

Directions:

1. Warm up your air fryer to 200°C.
2. Roll out puff pastry on your floured surface, then slice out six circles using a round cookie cutter or glass. Set aside.
3. In your pan on moderate temp, warm up some oil, then sauté shallot, garlic, plus mushrooms within 5 mins till softened.
4. Add cooked ham plus thyme leaves, then cook for another minute. Season the filling with salt plus pepper. Mix crème fraîche till just combined; set aside.
5. Using a smaller round cookie cutter or glass, create a well in four of the six pastry circles by cutting almost all the way through but leaving the bottom intact.
6. Leave at least half a centimetre around the edges of each circle.
7. Place the four circles with wells onto a parchment-lined air fryer tray or basket.
8. Divide the filling mixture evenly among these circles, pressing it slightly into the wells.
9. Close each pastry by placing one of the remaining uncut pastry circles on top, gently pressing down around the edges without letting any filling escape from the well.
10. Brush each vol-au-vent with beaten egg for glazing. Air fry pastries within 20-25 mins till puffed, checking on them at the half-way point to ensure even cooking. Serve.

Nutritional Values: Calories: 435; Carbs: 32g; Fat: 29g; Protein: 11g

Dutch Bitterballen Balls

Preparation time: 20 minutes + chilling time
Cooking time: 24 minutes
Servings: 4

Ingredients:

- 250g minced beef
- 30g butter
- 40g plain flour, plus extra for dusting
- 250ml beef stock
- One small onion, finely chopped
- Two garlic cloves, minced
- Half tsp freshly grated nutmeg
- Salt & black pepper, as required
- 50g breadcrumbs
- Two big eggs, beaten

Directions:

1. In your medium saucepan, dissolve butter on moderate temp. Put chopped onion plus garlic, then within 3 mins cook till softened.
2. Stir in flour to create a roux, cooking within 1 min.
3. Gradually add the beef stock while stirring continuously, ensuring there are no lumps. Cook within 5 mins till mixture thickens.
4. Add minced beef to the pan, breaking it up. Cook within 5 mins till browned.
5. Flavour with nutmeg, salt, plus black pepper. Remove, then allow to cool within 1 hour till chilled. Warm up your air fryer to 190°C.
6. Shape it into small balls (approximately golf ball-sized). Roll each ball in flour, dusting off any excess flour.
7. Coat each ball with beaten egg plus breadcrumbs.
8. Put bitterballen balls in your cooking basket, then cook within 15 mins till golden brown, turning once. Serve.
9. Carefully remove the bitterballen balls from the air fryer and serve with your favourite dipping sauce.

Nutritional Values: Calories: 442; Carbs: 23g; Fat: 29g; Protein: 25g

Polish Pierogi Dumplings

Preparation time: 45 minutes
Cooking time: 15 minutes
Servings: 4
Ingredients:

- 250g plain flour
- 120ml warm water
- One egg, beaten
- Half tsp salt
- 200g mashed potatoes
- 100g grated cheddar cheese
- One small onion, finely chopped
- Two tbsp butter, melted
- Salt & pepper, as required

Directions:

1. In your big container, mix flour, warm water, beaten egg, plus salt. Stir the mixture until a soft dough forms.
2. Knead it on your floured surface till elastic. Wrap in cling film, then let it rest within 30 mins.
3. In your separate container, mix mashed potatoes, grated cheddar cheese, plus chopped onion. Flavour with salt plus pepper.
4. Roll out the rested dough on your floured surface. Using a round cutter or glass, cut out circles of the dough.
5. Place a heaping tablespoon of filling onto each dough circle. Fold each circle in half, pinching the edges closed to form a pierogi shape. Be sure to seal well to prevent filling from leaking during cooking.

6. Warm up your air fryer to 190°C. Brush both sides of the pierogi with melted butter and arrange them in your cooking basket.
7. Cook pierogi within 6-8 mins on each side till golden brown. Serve.

Nutritional Values: Calories: 450; Carbs: 62g; Fat: 16g; Protein: 14g

Mini Prosciutto Quiches

Preparation time: 15 minutes
Cooking time: 12 minutes
Servings: 6
Ingredients:

- 100g diced prosciutto
- Six big free-range eggs
- 150ml double cream
- 60g grated mature Cheddar cheese
- One small leek, thinly sliced and washed (about 100g)
- Salt & ground black pepper, as required
- Cooking spray, for greasing

Directions:
1. Warm up your air fryer to 180°C and lightly spray a six-hole silicone muffin tray using cooking spray.
2. In your big container, mix eggs, double cream, grated Cheddar cheese, sliced leek, salt, plus black pepper.
3. Divide the diced prosciutto equally among the six muffin holes in the prepared tray.
4. Carefully pour the egg mixture into each muffin hole, filling them three-quarters full.
5. Place the filled tray into your cooking basket, then cook within 12 mins till quiches are puffed up. Serve.

Nutritional Values: Calories: 260; Carbs: 3g; Fat: 21g; Protein: 14g

Czech Fried Cheese Sticks

Preparation time: 10 minutes
Cooking time: 10 minutes
Servings: 4 people

Ingredients:

- 200g Edam or Gouda cheese, cut into 1cm thick sticks
- 50g plain flour
- One big egg, beaten
- 100g breadcrumbs
- Cooking spray or oil for the air fryer basket
- Salt & pepper, as required

Directions:
1. Prepare three shallow dishes. Place the flour in the first dish, the beaten egg in the second, and the breadcrumbs in the third dish.
2. Flavour both flour and beaten egg using salt plus pepper. Dip each cheese stick into the flour. Dip it into beaten egg mixture, then coat it evenly with breadcrumbs.
3. Warm up your air fryer to 200°C. Put breaded cheese sticks into your cooking basket.
4. Lightly brush cheese sticks with cooking oil. Cook within 10 mins till golden, flipping once. Serve.

Nutritional Values: Calories: 415; Carbs: 33g; Fat: 21g; Protein: 21g

Russian Blini with Smoked Salmon

Preparation time: 15 minutes
Cooking time: 8 minutes
Servings: 4

Ingredients:

- 100g plain flour
- Half tsp baking powder
- Salt, as required
- 150ml milk
- One big egg
- 50g unsalted butter, melted (plus extra for greasing)
- 200g smoked salmon, thinly sliced
- Fresh dill, to serve
- Sour cream or crème fraîche, to serve

Directions:

1. In your container, combine the plain flour, baking powder, plus salt.
2. In your separate container, whisk milk plus egg till well combined. Combine it with dry mixture till smooth. Stir in the melted butter until fully incorporated.
3. Warm up your air fryer to 180°C. Lightly grease your cooking basket using some extra butter.
4. Spoon small dollops of batter (about a tablespoon each) onto the greased air fryer basket, leaving enough space between them for expansion.
5. Cook blinis in batches for around 4 mins per side till golden brown. Repeat for the remaining batter.
6. Top each blini with sour cream or crème fraîche, a slice of smoked salmon, and a sprig of fresh dill.

Nutritional Values: Calories: 371; Carbs: 23g; Fat: 22g; Protein: 21g

Savoury French Gougères

Preparation time: 15 minutes
Cooking time: 20-25 minutes
Servings: 8

Ingredients:

- 250ml water
- 100g unsalted butter, diced
- 150g plain flour
- Half tsp salt
- Half tsp mustard powder
- Four big eggs, lightly beaten
- 150g Gruyère cheese, grated
- ground black pepper, as required

Directions:

1. Warm up your air fryer to 180°C.
2. In your medium saucepan, mix water plus butter on moderate temp till butter has melted. Remove.
3. Put plain flour, salt, plus mustard powder, then stir vigorously till smooth. Adjust to low temp, then cook within one min, stirring till dough forms a ball.
4. Transfer it into your big container, then let it cool. Gradually add eggs while mixing with an electric mixer until fully incorporated.
5. Fold in grated Gruyère cheese, then flavour with black pepper.
6. Line your air fryer basket with parchment paper. Using a piping bag or spoon, form small rounds of dough about the size of walnuts onto the parchment paper in your air fryer basket (make sure to leave space between them for expansion).
7. Air fry at 180°C within 20-25 mins till puffed up. Make sure not to open the air fryer during cooking, as this may cause the gougères to deflate. Serve.

Nutritional Values: Calories: 295; Carbs: 20g; Fat: 19g; Protein: 11g

Shrimp Escabeche Skewers

Preparation time: 15 minutes + marinating time
Cooking time: 9 minutes
Servings: 4

Ingredients:
- 450g raw king prawns, shelled & deveined
- Two medium carrots, thinly sliced
- One small red onion, sliced into thin wedges
- One small red bell pepper, sliced into bite-sized pieces
- 120ml apple cider vinegar
- 60ml extra virgin olive oil
- Juice of one lemon
- Zest of one lemon
- Two garlic cloves, minced
- Salt & black pepper, as required

Directions:
1. In your big container, whisk apple cider vinegar, olive oil, lemon juice, lemon zest, minced garlic, salt plus black pepper. Put aside.
2. Thread the prawns onto wooden skewers along with carrots, onion wedges and red bell pepper pieces, alternating between each ingredient.
3. Put prepared skewers in your shallow container, then pour escabeche marinade. Marinate within 30 mins.
4. Warm up your air fryer to 180°C. Remove the shrimp skewers from the marinade, then let any excess marinade drip off. Reserve leftover marinade for later use.
5. Put marinated shrimp skewers in your cooking basket. Cook within 4 mins per side till prawns turn pink.
6. While cooking shrimp skewers, transfer remaining marinade to your small saucepan, then boil on moderate temp within one minute to create a serving sauce.
7. Serve shrimp skewers hot with boiled marinade as a dipping sauce.

Nutritional Values: Calories: 320; Carbs: 10g; Fat: 17g; Protein: 31g

Easy Veggie Samosas

Preparation time: 30 minutes
Cooking time: 28 minutes
Servings: 4

Ingredients:
- 240g plain flour
- 120ml cold water
- Two tsp vegetable oil, plus extra for brushing
- One medium onion, finely chopped
- One medium carrot, grated
- 100g frozen peas, thawed
- One medium potato, boiled and diced
- One tsp each cumin seeds & ground coriander
- Half tsp each turmeric & garam masala
- Salt, as required

Directions:
1. In your big container, mix flour, water plus salt. Knead to form a soft dough. Cover using damp cloth, then put aside within 20 mins.
2. Meanwhile, warm up vegetable oil in your pan on moderate temp. Put onion, then cook within 3 to 4 mins till softened. Stir in grated carrot plus peas.
3. Cook within few mins till vegetables are tender.
4. Add boiled potatoes, cumin seeds, ground coriander, turmeric, garam masala plus salt. Stir well till heated through.

5. Divide dough into four, then roll each portion into a ball. Roll out each ball into a thin circle about six inches in diameter.
6. Cut each circle in half and form a cone shape by folding one side over the other with a little water to seal.
7. Fill each cone with two tablespoons of veggie mixture before gently sealing the edges shut by pinching together. Warm up your air fryer to 180°C.
8. Brush each samosa lightly using oil, then place no more than four at a time in your cooking basket. Cook within 25 mins till golden brown. Serve.

Nutritional Values: Calories: 310; Carbs: 60g; Fat: 4g; Protein: 8g

Bacon-Wrapped Dates

Preparation time: 10 minutes
Cooking time: 10 minutes
Servings: 6

Ingredients:
- 18 pitted dates
- Six rashers of streaky bacon, cut into thirds

Directions:
1. Warm up your air fryer to 200°C.
2. Wrap each date with a third of a bacon rasher, making sure the bacon is securely wrapped around the date. If necessary, use toothpicks to secure bacon.
3. Put wrapped dates on your cooking basket. Cook within 5 mins, flip them over then cook within 5 mins till bacon is crispy. Serve.

Nutritional Values: Calories: 185; Carbs: 18g; Fat: 10g; Protein: 5g

DESSERTS & SWEET TREATS

French Raspberry Meringue Tarts

Preparation time: 30 minutes
Cooking time: 22 minutes
Servings: 6

Ingredients:

- 150g plain flour
- 75g unsalted butter, chilled and diced
- Three tbsp icing sugar, plus more for dusting
- One big egg yolk
- One tbsp cold water
- 200g fresh raspberries
- Three big egg whites
- 150g caster sugar

Directions:

1. In your big container, mix plain flour plus diced butter till it resembles fine breadcrumbs. Stir in the icing sugar.
2. Put egg yolk plus cold water, then mix till a dough forms. Wrap the dough, then chill within 15 mins. Warm up your air fryer to 180°C.
3. Roll out dough between two sheets of parchment paper to a thickness of about 0.5cm.
4. Cut out six circles with a pastry cutter or glass, then press each dough circle into a greased tart tin.
5. Prick the bottoms of each tart using your fork, then blind bake using baking beans in your air fryer within 12 mins till lightly golden. Remove, then let them cool down.
6. Meanwhile, make the meringue by beating together egg whites till stiff peaks form, adding caster sugar while whisking continuously.
7. Fill each tart crust with raspberries, leaving a small space on top for the meringue.
8. Pipe or spoon the meringue mixture onto each raspberry-filled tart, completely covering them.
9. Bake tarts in your preheated air fryer at 160°C within 10-13 mins till meringue is lightly golden.
10. Remove tarts, then let them cool down before dusting with icing sugar. Serve.

Nutritional Values: Calories: 344; Carbs: 56g; Fat: 11g; Protein: 6g

German Schokokuchen Bites

Preparation time: 15 minutes
Cooking time: 12 minutes
Servings: 9

Ingredients:

- 150g dark chocolate, chopped
- 120g unsalted butter, softened
- 80g caster sugar
- Three medium eggs
- 70g self-raising flour
- 20g cocoa powder
- One-fourth tsp salt

Directions:

1. Warm up your air fryer to 180°C.

2. In your heat-proof container, melt the chopped dark chocolate using a microwave or a double boiler. Set aside to cool slightly.
3. In your separate big container, cream softened butter plus caster sugar till fluffy.
4. Gradually add eggs one at a time, whisking well between each addition.
5. Gently fold in the melted chocolate until fully incorporated into the mixture.
6. Sift in the self-raising flour, cocoa powder, plus salt, then carefully stir till just combined, ensuring no dry pockets remain. Do not overmix.
7. Place teaspoon-sized dollops of batter into silicone mini-muffin moulds or lined air fryer-safe muffin cups to create bite-sized portions, filling them about two-thirds full.
8. Transfer filled moulds to your air fryer, then cook within 12 mins till firm. Serve.

Nutritional Values: Calories: 329; Carbs: 27g; Fat: 21g; Protein: 5g

English Sticky Toffee Puddings

Preparation time: 20 minutes
Cooking time: 15 minutes
Servings: 6

Ingredients:
- 200g pitted dates, chopped
- 250ml boiling water
- One tsp bicarbonate of soda
- 60g unsalted butter, softened
- 150g light muscovado sugar
- Two big eggs
- 180g self-raising flour
- Salt, as required
- For the toffee sauce:
- 200ml double cream
- 100g unsalted butter
- 100g light muscovado sugar

Directions:

1. In your heatproof container, mix chopped dates, boiling water, plus bicarbonate of soda.
Set aside for about 10 minutes to allow the dates to soften.
2. In your separate big container, cream butter plus sugar till fluffy. Add eggs one at a time, mixing thoroughly after each addition.
3. Gradually fold in the self-raising flour plus salt. Stir in softened date mixture until fully combined.
4. Warm up your air fryer to 180°C. Grease six individual ramekins or pudding moulds. Divide pudding batter evenly among each.
5. Put ramekins in your cooking basket, ensuring they are not overcrowded, and cook within 15 mins till firm.
6. Meanwhile, prepare toffee sauce by heating the double cream, unsalted butter, and muscovado sugar in your small saucepan on moderate temp till smooth. Remove, then put aside.
7. Drizzle each pudding generously with the warm toffee sauce.

Nutritional Values: Calories: 695; Carbs: 92g; Fat: 34g; Protein: 8g

Italian Air-fried Cannoli

Preparation time: 20 minutes + chilling time
Cooking time: 8 minutes
Servings: 12 cannoli

Ingredients:
- 250g plain flour
- 30g white sugar
- One tsp cocoa powder
- Half tsp ground cinnamon
- 60g unsalted butter, chilled and cubed
- 60ml dry Marsala wine
- 800g ricotta cheese, drained
- 150g icing sugar, + extra for dusting
- One tsp vanilla extract
- 65g mini chocolate chips or currants

Directions:
1. In your container, mix plain flour, white sugar, cocoa powder, and ground cinnamon. Put cubed unsalted butter, then use your fingers to rub it into the dry mixture until it resembles breadcrumbs.
2. Slowly add the Marsala wine while stirring until a dough forms. Cover in cling film and refrigerate for at least 30 minutes.
3. In another container, whisk ricotta cheese, icing sugar, plus vanilla extract till smooth. Fold in the chocolate chips or currants. Refrigerate until assembly.
4. Preheat your air fryer to 180°C.
5. Roll out refrigerated dough to about a 3mm thickness on your floured surface. Cut out twelve circles using a round cookie cutter or drinking glass (around 10cm diameter).
6. Wrap each dough circle around a cannoli mould, overlapping the edges slightly and sealing with water.
7. Put cannoli onto your cooking basket, then cook within 8 mins till golden brown. Use tongs to carefully remove each cooked cannoli from its mould and set aside on your wire rack to cool.
8. Once cooled, fill each cannoli shell with the ricotta mixture using a piping bag or even a ziplock bag with the corner snipped off.
9. Dust the finished cannoli with a liberal sprinkling of icing sugar before serving.

Nutritional Values: Calories: 425; Carbs: 47g; Fat: 20g; Protein: 11g

Greek Loukoumades with Honey

Preparation time: 15 minutes
Cooking time: 10 minutes
Servings: 4-6

Ingredients:
- 250g plain flour
- One tsp instant yeast
- Half tsp salt
- 250ml warm water
- One tbsp caster sugar
- Vegetable oil, for greasing air fryer tray
- 150g honey
- 50g walnuts, chopped
- Ground cinnamon, to taste

Directions:
1. In your big container, mix plain flour, instant yeast, plus salt. Slowly pour warm water while stirring till smooth.
2. Cover, then set in a warm location within 1 hour to allow the batter to ferment and rise.
3. Warm up your air fryer to 180°C. Lightly oil your cooking tray using vegetable oil.
4. With a small spoon or ice cream scoop, form small balls of dough and place them onto the greased cooking tray.
5. Cook dough balls within 10 mins till golden brown, turning them once.
6. As the loukoumades cook, prepare a honey syrup by gently warming the honey in your small saucepan on low temp till it becomes runny.
7. Transfer loukoumades to your serving plate, then drizzle with warmed honey syrup.
8. Top with chopped walnuts and finish off with a sprinkle of ground cinnamon.

Nutritional Values: Calories: 497; Carbs: 68g; Fat: 8g; Protein: 11g

Dutch Stroopwafel Crisps

Preparation time: 15 minutes
Cooking time: 5 minutes
Servings: 6

Ingredients:

- 100g plain flour
- One-fourth tsp baking powder
- 65g caster sugar
- Salt, as required
- 50g unsalted butter, melted
- One medium egg
- One tsp vanilla extract
- 100g golden syrup (for filling)
- 50g light brown sugar (for filling)
- 50g unsalted butter (for filling)
- Half tsp ground cinnamon (for filling)

Directions:

1. In your big container, mix plain flour, baking powder, caster sugar, plus salt.
2. Add melted unsalted butter, whisked egg, plus vanilla extract. Stir until well combined. Warm up your air fryer to 180°C.
3. Roll out dough on your floured surface till it's about 2 mm thick.
4. Use a round cookie cutter to cut out circles from the dough. Re-roll any excess dough and cut more circles until all the dough is used up.
5. Place half of the circles on a lined cooking tray, then cook within 3 to 4 mins till crisp, flipping once. Repeat with rest of dough circles.
6. In your small saucepan on low temp, prepare filling by combining golden syrup, light brown sugar, unsalted butter, and ground cinnamon. Stir occasionally until well combined and heated through.
7. Spread a layer of the warm filling onto one side of each cooked wafer and immediately press another wafer onto it, creating your stroopwafel crisps.

Nutritional Values: Calories: 324; Carbs: 42g; Fat: 17g; Protein: 4g

Scottish Cranachan Parfaits

Preparation time: 15 minutes
Cooking time: 3 minutes
Servings: 4
Ingredients:

- 250g raspberries
- Two tbsp Scottish whisky
- Three tbsp honey
- 300ml double cream
- 100g jumbo oats
- 50g chopped almonds

Directions:

1. In your container, mix raspberries, whisky, plus 2 tablespoons of honey. Put aside for 10 minutes to allow the flavours to infuse.
2. Warm up your air fryer to 180°C.
3. In your separate container, mix jumbo oats and chopped almonds. Spread this mixture evenly in your cooking basket, then cook within 3 mins, then give the mixture a good shake and cook within 3 mins till golden brown. Remove, then let cool.
4. In another container, whisk double cream till soft peaks. Gently fold in remaining tablespoon of honey.
5. Assemble your cranachan parfaits by dividing half of the raspberry mixture between four individual serving glasses.
6. Spoon half of whipped cream on top, followed by a layer of the oat and almond mixture.
7. Repeat layering using rest of raspberry mixture, whipped cream, and oat-almond mixture. Serve.

Nutritional Values: Calories: 587; Carbs: 44g; Fat: 41g; Protein: 9g

Danish Kransekage Rings

Preparation time: 30 minutes
Cooking time: 7 minutes
Servings: 8

Ingredients:
- 450g ground almonds
- 400g icing sugar
- Three egg whites (at room temperature)
- One tsp almond extract
- Zest of half a lemon
- Salt, as required
- 50g plain flour (for rolling)
- Cooking spray (for greasing the air fryer)

Directions:
1. In your big container, mix ground almonds plus icing sugar. In your separate container, whisk egg whites till soft peaks.
2. Gradually fold whisked egg whites into almond mixture, along with almond extract, lemon zest, plus salt. Combine until it forms a firm dough.
3. Sprinkle plain flour on your working surface, then divide dough into three.
4. Roll each part into long ropes of approx. 40 cm in length and tapering towards the ends.
5. Form each rope into an oval-shaped ring and press lightly to join at the ends. The rings should be in graduating sizes from large to small.
6. Place a sheet of baking paper in your cooking basket and lightly oil it using cooking spray. Warm up your air fryer at 190°C.
7. Gently transfer the rings to your cooking basket. Cook within 7 mins at 190°C till golden brown.
8. Remove, then let it cool completely before stacking from largest to smallest. To serve, drizzle with icing sugar or melted chocolate if desired.

Nutritional Values: Calories: 462; Carbs: 53g; Fat: 24g; Protein: 12g

Austrian Sacher Torte Cake

Preparation time: 20 minutes
Cooking time: 30 minutes
Servings: 10

Ingredients:
- 170g unsalted butter, softened
- 150g caster sugar
- Six big eggs, separated
- 180g dark chocolate, melted and cooled
- 140g plain flour, sifted
- One tbsp each cocoa powder & baking powder
- Half tsp salt
- 150g apricot jam, for filling

For the glaze:
- 200g dark chocolate, finely chopped
- 125ml double cream

Directions:
1. Warm up air fryer to 160°C. Grease your round cake tin (20cm), then line using baking parchment.
2. In your big container, cream butter plus sugar till fluffy. Add egg yolks one at a time, beating well after each addition. Mix in melted chocolate.
3. In another container, whisk egg whites till stiff peaks. Fold into chocolate mixture.

4. Sift flour, cocoa powder, baking powder, plus salt. Fold into chocolate mixture till well combined.
5. Pour batter into your cake tin, then put in your cooking basket. Cook within 25 mins till it sets. Cool it down.
6. Once cooled, slice cake horizontally into two layers. Spread apricot jam between layers, then sandwich together.

For the glaze:

7. Put chopped chocolate in your heatproof container.
8. In your small saucepan, warm up double cream till it just begins to simmer. Pour hot cream over chocolate, then let it sit within 2 mins. Stir till chocolate is melted.
9. Pour glaze over cake, allowing it to run down sides. Use a palette knife to spread glaze evenly. Serve.

Nutritional Values: Calories: 538; Carbs: 54g; Fat: 33g; Protein: 9g

Norwegian Lefse Bites

Preparation time: 20 minutes
Cooking time: 10 minutes
Servings: 6

Ingredients:

- 250g mashed potatoes
- 60g plain flour
- One tbsp granulated sugar
- Half tsp salt
- 40g butter, melted
- Cinnamon-sugar mixture for sprinkling (2 tbsp granulated sugar combined with 1 tsp cinnamon)

Directions:

1. In your big container, mix mashed potatoes, plain flour, granulated sugar, plus salt. Add melted butter, then mix well till a smooth dough forms.
2. On your floured surface, roll out dough into a rectangle shape. Trim any uneven edges.
3. Sprinkle a generous amount of the cinnamon-sugar mixture evenly over the rolled-out dough.
4. Carefully roll up the dough from one long edge to create a tight log.
5. Cut the log into bite-sized pieces, approximately 1 inch thick, and arrange on a plate or tray. Warm up your air fryer to 180°C.
6. Put lefse bites in your cooking basket, then air fry within 10 mins golden brown, flipping once. Cool it down. Serve.

Nutritional Values: Calories: 190; Carbs: 30g; Fat: 6g; Protein: 3g

Swedish Almond Kardemummabulle

Preparation time: 20 minutes
Cooking time: 12 minutes
Servings: 8

Ingredients:

- 400g plain flour
- 50g caster sugar
- One tsp ground kardemumma (cardamom)
- 14g instant yeast
- 240ml whole milk, lukewarm
- 60g unsalted butter, melted
- One big egg, slightly beaten
- Salt, as required

Filling:

- 100g unsalted butter, softened
- 100g caster sugar
- One tbsp ground cinnamon
- One tsp ground kardemumma (cardamom)
- 100g almond paste, grated

For the Glaze:

- Apricot jam, warmed and sieved

Directions:

1. In your big container, mix plain flour, caster sugar, ground kardemumma, instant yeast, plus salt.
2. Add the lukewarm whole milk and melted unsalted butter. Stir till combined.

3. Mix in slightly beaten egg and knead into a smooth dough on your floured surface.
4. Put dough in your greased container, then cover using clean tea towel. Allow to rise for an hour in a warm place.
5. Meanwhile, prepare the filling by mixing together the softened unsalted butter, caster sugar, ground cinnamon, ground kardemumma (cardamom), and grated almond paste.
6. Once the dough has risen, roll it out into a large rectangle on a floured surface. Spread filling evenly over dough.
7. Gently roll up dough lengthwise into a log shape. Slice into eight even pieces.
8. Warm up your air fryer to 180°C. Put rolls in your cooking basket, then cook within 12 mins till golden brown.
9. Allow Kardemummabulle to cool, then brush each roll with the warmed apricot jam. Serve.

Nutritional Values: Calories: 534; Carbs: 76g; Fat: 22g; Protein: 11g

Icelandic Skyr Cheesecake Cups

Preparation time: 15 minutes + chilling time
Cooking time: 20 minutes
Servings: 6

Ingredients:

- 250g digestive biscuits
- 100g unsalted butter, melted
- 450g Icelandic Skyr (or substitute Greek yoghurt)
- 200g full-fat cream cheese
- 150g granulated sugar
- Two big eggs
- One tsp vanilla extract
- Zest of one lemon
- Salt, as required

Directions:

1. In your food processor, crush digestive biscuits until they are fine crumbs. Pour butter, then pulse till well combined.
2. Press about two tablespoons of the mixture into the bottom of each silicone cupcake liner.
3. Warm up your air fryer to 160°C. Ensure that silicone cupcake liners fit into your air fryer basket before proceeding.
4. In your big container, whisk Skyr, cream cheese, sugar, eggs, vanilla, lemon zest, and salt till smooth.
5. Spoon the cheesecake mixture into each cupcake liners, filling each one to about three-quarters full.
6. Place filled silicone cupcake liners into your cooking basket. Cook at 160°C within 18-20 mins till cheesecakes are set.
7. Cool it down, then chill in your refrigerator within 2 hours. Once chilled, carefully remove the cheesecake cups from their silicone liners and serve.

Nutritional Values: Calories: 415; Carbs: 36g; Fat: 24g; Protein: 12g

Czech Trdelník Twists

Preparation time: 20 minutes + rising time
Cooking time: 12 minutes
Servings: 8 twists

Ingredients:

- 500g plain flour
- 7g fast-action dried yeast
- 250ml warm milk
- 75g caster sugar
- One tsp salt
- One big egg, beaten
- Two tbsp melted unsalted butter
- 200g granulated sugar, for coating
- Two tsp ground cinnamon, for coating

Directions:

1. In your big container, mix flour plus yeast. Add warm milk, caster sugar, plus salt, mixing until well combined.
2. Add beaten egg plus melted butter. Stir till a smooth dough is formed. Cover, then let it rest within 1 hour in a warm place.
3. Once the dough has doubled in size, divide it into eight equal pieces. Roll out each piece into thin strips approximately 60cm in length.
4. Grease your cooking basket using cooking spray.
5. Twist two strips together to create a spiral shape, pinching the ends together to prevent it from unraveling during cooking.
6. In a shallow dish, mix the granulated sugar and ground cinnamon for coating.
7. Roll each twisted pair of dough strips in the cinnamon sugar mixture, ensuring all sides are coated evenly.
8. Warm up your air fryer to 180°C. Place two coated trdelník twists at a time in your cooking basket.
9. Cook within 6 mins on one side, then then flip them over using tongs to cook within 6 mins till golden brown.
10. Repeat with the remaining trdelník twists. Allow the trdelník twists to cool for a few minutes before enjoying with hot chocolate, coffee, or tea.

Nutritional Values: Calories: 470; Carbs: 69g; Fat: 8g; Protein: 12g

Hungarian Dobos Torte Rolls

Preparation time: 20 minutes
Cooking time: 12 minutes
Servings: 6

Ingredients:

- 150g caster sugar
- Four big eggs, separated
- 120g plain flour
- One tsp baking powder
- Salt, as required
- 60ml whole milk
- Two tsp vanilla extract
- 300g unsalted butter, softened
- 200g icing sugar
- One tbsp cocoa powder
- 100g dark chocolate, melted

Directions:

1. In your big container, beat caster sugar plus egg yolks till fluffy. Then gently fold in sifted plain flour, baking powder, and a pinch of salt.
2. In your separate container, whisk egg whites to form stiff peaks. Gently fold egg whites into flour mixture till well combined.
3. Gradually add whole milk and vanilla extract to the batter, stirring until smooth.
4. Warm up your air fryer to 180°C. Line your air fryer-safe baking tray using parchment paper.
5. Drop spoonfuls of batter onto the prepared baking tray, about 6cm apart. Smooth the batter to create even circles for each roll.
6. Put tray in your air fryer, then cook within 12 mins till golden brown.

7. While the rolls are cooking, prepare the filling by beating together unsalted butter and icing sugar until creamy. Stir in cocoa powder plus dark chocolate.
8. Once the rolls have cooled, spread a generous amount of filling on each roll and gently roll them into a spiral shape. Serve.

Nutritional Values: Calories: 465; Carbs: 63g; Fat: 25g; Protein: 9g

Croatian Air-fried Fritule

Preparation time: 15 minutes
Cooking time: 10 minutes
Servings: 4

Ingredients:
- 200g plain flour
- 50g granulated sugar
- One tsp baking powder
- One-fourth tsp salt
- One big egg
- 120ml plain yoghurt
- Two tbsp vegetable oil
- One tsp vanilla extract
- Zest of one lemon
- Zest of one orange

Directions:
1. In your big container, mix flour, sugar, baking powder, plus salt.
2. In your separate container, whisk egg, yoghurt, vegetable oil, plus vanilla extract. Combine it with dry mixture. Fold in the lemon plus orange zest.
3. Warm up your air fryer to 180°C. Lightly oil your cooking basket using a bit of oil.
4. Using a spoon or your hands, shape small dough balls, then put them in your cooking basket.
5. Cook within 10 mins till golden brown, shaking your basket once. Serve.

Nutritional Values: Calories: 398; Carbs: 62g; Fat: 12g; Protein: 10g

Romanian Air-fried Papanasi

Preparation time: 15 minutes
Cooking time: 10 minutes
Servings: 4

Ingredients:
- 250g plain flour
- One tsp baking powder
- Salt, as required
- Two big free-range eggs
- 50g caster sugar
- 250g cottage cheese
- Zest of one lemon
- One tsp pure vanilla extract
- Vegetable oil, for brushing the air fryer basket

For serving:
- 150g soured cream
- 150g berry jam (preferably lingonberry or blackcurrant)

Directions:
1. In your big container, mix flour, baking powder, plus salt. Put aside.
2. In your separate container, beat eggs plus sugar till fluffy. Stir in cottage cheese, lemon zest and vanilla extract until well combined.
3. Combine it with dry mixture till a smooth dough forms. Beware not to overmix.
4. Divide it into eight, then form each into a ball.
5. Working with one ball at a time, create a doughnut shape by pressing your thumb into the centre of the ball to make an indentation.

Elongate the hole slightly for better results after frying.
6. Warm up your air fryer to 180°C.
7. Brush your cooking basket using vegetable oil, then put four papanasi at a time into it, ensuring they're not touching each other.
8. Cook at 180°C for about ten minutes, gently flipping halfway through until evenly golden-brown.
9. Remove cooked papanasi from the air fryer using tongs and repeat steps with remaining papanasi. Serve with soured cream and berry on top.

Nutritional Values: Calories: 575; Carbs: 74g; Fat: 14g; Protein: 22g

Serbian Almond Plazma Cookies

Preparation time: 15 minutes
Cooking time: 8 minutes
Servings: 24 cookies

Ingredients:
- 200g Plazma biscuits, crushed
- 100g ground almonds
- 150ml milk
- 50g unsalted butter, melted
- Half tsp almond extract
- 100g granulated sugar
- One egg white, lightly beaten

Directions:
1. In your big container, mix crushed Plazma biscuits, ground almonds, milk, melted butter, almond extract, and granulated sugar. Mix well until a dough is formed.
2. Warm up your air fryer to 180°C. Using your hands, roll tablespoon-sized portions of dough into balls, then put them on your plate.
3. Flatten each ball with the palm of your hand and shape the cookies into neat circles. If desired, press a few flaked almonds onto the top of each cookie for decoration.
4. Line your cooking basket using parchment paper, then put shaped cookies in your cooking basket.
5. Cook within 8 mins till golden brown on top but still soft in the centre. Serve.

Nutritional Values: Calories: 110; Carbs: 13g; Fat: 5g; Protein: 2g

Bulgarian Medenki Honey Biscuits

Preparation time: 20 minutes + chilling time
Cooking time: 6 minutes
Servings: 24 biscuits

Ingredients:
- 100g unsalted butter, softened
- 115g caster sugar
- Two big eggs (1 for the dough and 1 for glazing)
- 80ml honey
- 360g plain flour
- One tsp each baking soda, ground cinnamon & ground cloves

Directions:
1. In your big container, cream softened butter plus caster sugar till light.
2. Add one egg to the mixture, followed by the honey. Mix well to combine.
3. In your separate container, whisk plain flour, baking soda, ground cinnamon, plus ground cloves.

4. Combine it with butter mixture, stirring to form a smooth dough. Wrap, then refrigerate within 1 hour.
5. Warm up your air fryer to 180°C. Meanwhile, roll out chilled dough on your floured surface to about 4mm thick.
6. Using a biscuit cutter, cut out your desired shapes and carefully transfer them onto a sheet of baking paper that fits within your air fryer basket or tray.
7. Beat rest of egg and gently apply it to each biscuit as a glaze. Put biscuits into your cooking basket. Cook within 6 mins till golden brown. Serve.

Nutritional Values: Calories: 129; Carbs: 20g; Fat: 4g; Protein: 2g

Maltese Date-Filled Maqrut

Preparation time: 20 minutes
Cooking time: 25 minutes
Servings: 6

Ingredients:
- 250g plain flour
- 125g cold unsalted butter, cubed
- 50g icing sugar
- One-fourth tsp salt
- 50ml cold water
- 350g pitted dates, chopped
- 100ml hot water
- Zest of one lemon
- Half tsp ground cinnamon
- A pinch of ground cloves
- Oil spray for air frying

Directions:
1. In your big container, mix flour, cold butter, icing sugar, plus salt. Use your fingers to gently rub the mixture till it resembles coarse crumbs.
2. Slowly pour cold water to form soft dough. Wrap, then refrigerate within one hour.
3. Meanwhile, prepare the date filling by combining the pitted dates, hot water, lemon zest, cinnamon, plus cloves in your saucepan.
4. Simmer on low temp within 10 mins till dates are soft and have absorbed most of the water. Remove, then cool before forming filling into six equal portions.
5. Warm up your air fryer to 180°C.
6. On your floured surface, divide chilled dough into six, then roll each piece into a rectangular shape about half centimetre thick.
7. Put date filling on each dough rectangle and fold the dough over to enclose it completely. Press gently on edges to seal.
8. Slice each filled rectangle into five Maqrut shaped diamond pieces. Lightly oil your cooking basket, then add Maqrut pieces.
9. Air fry within 15 mins till golden brown, turning them once. Serve.

Nutritional Values: Calories: 357; Carbs: 65g; Fat: 9g; Protein: 5g

Italian Tiramisu Cups

Preparation time: 20 minutes + chilling time
Cooking time: 10 minutes
Servings: 4

Ingredients:

- Four big eggs, yolks & whites separated
- 100g caster sugar
- 250g mascarpone cheese
- 200ml strong coffee, cooled
- 100ml Marsala wine (optional)
- 12 sponge fingers (savoiardi)
- Cocoa powder, for dusting
- Grated dark chocolate, for garnishing

Directions:

1. In your big container, whisk egg yolks plus sugar till creamy. Add mascarpone cheese, whisking until smooth and well combined.
2. In your separate container, whisk egg whites till stiff peaks. Fold whisked whites into mascarpone mixture.
3. Mix cooled coffee and Marsala wine (if using) in your shallow container. Briefly dip each sponge finger into mixture, ensuring they are moist but not soggy.
4. Arrange four ramekins on your work surface. Place one soaked sponge finger in each ramekin and then layer with a spoonful of mascarpone mix.
5. Repeat step to create two layers of soaked sponge fingers and mascarpone.
6. Warm up your air fryer to 160°C. Cover tiramisu cups in foil, then place them in your cooking basket. Cook within 10 mins till set.
7. Remove, cool it down, then chill within 2 hours. Before serving, dust each tiramisu cup with cocoa powder and garnish with grated dark chocolate.

Nutritional Values: Calories: 560; Carbs: 54g; Fat: 32g; Protein: 13g

Victoria Sponge Cake Bites

Preparation time: 20 minutes
Cooking time: 10 minutes
Servings: 20 bites

Ingredients:

- 200g self-raising flour
- 200g unsalted butter, softened
- 200g caster sugar
- Four medium eggs, beaten
- One tsp baking powder
- Two tsp vanilla extract
- 100g strawberry or raspberry jam
- 200ml double cream
- Icing sugar, for dusting

Directions:

1. In your big container, mix softened butter plus caster sugar. Beat till fluffy. Gradually add beaten eggs, mixing well after each addition.
2. Sift self-raising flour plus baking powder. Gently fold in until fully combined. Stir in the vanilla extract. Warm up your air fryer to 190°C.
3. Grease an air fryer parchment liner or cake bites mould (if using), then spoon one tablespoon of batter into each section/mould.
4. Cook within 10 mins till golden brown. Cool it down.
5. Once cooled, slice each cake bite horizontally in half, taking care not to break them apart.
6. Whip double cream till stiff peaks form, then spread a dollop of jam followed by a spoonful of whipped cream on the bottom half of each cake bite.
7. Gently press the top half onto the jam and cream layer. Dust with icing sugar before serving.

Nutritional Values: Calories: 190; Carbs: 19g; Fat: 11g; Protein: 3g

Hungarian Dobos Torte Squares

Preparation time: 40 minutes
Cooking time: 20 minutes
Servings: 9 squares

Ingredients:
- 200g unsalted butter, softened
- 150g caster sugar
- Four big eggs, separated
- One tsp vanilla extract
- 200g plain flour
- One tsp baking powder
- Salt, as required
- 100g dark chocolate, chopped
- 300ml double cream
- 150g icing sugar, sifted
- One tbsp cocoa powder

Directions:
1. In your container, cream softened butter plus caster sugar till fluffy. Add egg yolks plus vanilla extract, then mix well.
2. In your separate container, mix plain flour, baking powder, plus salt. Combine it with wet mixture. Put aside.
3. Using an electric mixer, whisk egg whites to stiff peaks. Fold egg whites into cake batter till well combined.
4. Warm up your air fryer to 160°C. Oil your 20cm x 20cm square cake tin, then line it using baking paper. Pour batter into your tin, smoothing out the surface.
5. Put tin in your cooking basket, then cook within 18-20 mins till it sets. Cool it down.
6. Meanwhile, for chocolate ganache, warm up double cream in your saucepan on low temp till it just begins to simmer.
7. Remove, then add chopped dark chocolate, stirring continuously until smooth and glossy.
8. In another container, whisk icing sugar plus cocoa powder. Add the cooled chocolate ganache and mix to form a spreadable consistency.
9. Once the cake has cooled, cut it into 9 equal squares. Spread a generous layer of the chocolate icing over each square.

Nutritional Values: Calories: 512; Carbs: 58g; Fat: 30g; Protein: 7g

Swiss Nut and Chocolate Meringues

Preparation time: 20 minutes
Cooking time: 30 minutes
Servings: 12 meringues
Ingredients:
- Four big egg whites (at room temperature)
- 200g caster sugar
- One tsp white wine vinegar
- One tsp cornflour
- 100g dark chocolate, finely chopped
- 100g mixed nuts (such as hazelnuts and almonds, roughly chopped)

Directions:
1. In your clean, dry container, whisk egg whites till stiff peaks form.
2. Add caster sugar, a tbsp at a time, whisking till meringue mixture is glossy and thick.
3. Gently fold in the white wine vinegar and cornflour just until incorporated.
4. Carefully fold in the chopped dark chocolate and mixed nuts so they are evenly distributed.
5. Warm up your air fryer to 100°C.
6. Line your cooking basket using parchment paper and spoon mounded dollops of the meringue mixture onto it, spaced apart to allow for expansion during cooking.
7. Cook within 30 mins till meringues are crisp. Cool it down. Serve.

Nutritional Values: Calories: 159; Carbs: 19g; Fat: 7g; Protein: 3g

COOKING CONVERSION CHART

Volume Equivalents (Liquid)

US STANDARD	US STANDARD (OUNCES)	METRIC (APPROXIMATE)
2 tablespoons	1 fl. oz.	30 mL
¼ cup	2 fl. oz.	60 mL
½ cup	4 fl. oz.	120 mL
1 cup	8 fl. oz.	240 mL
1½ cups	12 fl. oz.	355 mL
2 cups or 1 pint	16 fl. oz.	475 mL
4 cups or 1 quart	32 fl. oz.	1 L
1 gallon	128 fl. oz.	4 L

Volume Equivalents (Dry)

US STANDARD	METRIC (APPROXIMATE)
⅛ teaspoon	0.5 mL
¼ teaspoon	1 mL
½ teaspoon	2 mL
¾ teaspoon	4 mL
1 teaspoon	5 mL
1 tablespoon	15 mL
¼ cup	59 mL
⅓ cup	79 mL
½ cup	118 mL
⅔ cup	156 mL
¾ cup	177 mL
1 cup	235 mL
2 cups or 1 pint	475 mL
3 cups	700 mL
4 cups or 1 quart	1 L
½ gallon	2 L
1 gallon	4 L

Oven Temperatures

FAHRENHEIT (F)	CELSIUS (C) (APPROXIMATE)
250	120
300	150
325	165
350	180
375	190
400	200
425	220
450	230

Weight Equivalents

US STANDARD	METRIC (APPROXIMATE)
½ ounce	15 g
1 ounce	30 g
2 ounces	60 g
4 ounces	115 g
8 ounces	225 g
12 ounces	340 g
16 ounces or 1 pound	455 g

CONCLUSION

Air Fryers has genuinely revolutionised our home kitchens, offering an array of mouth-watering recipes ideal for British gastronomes seeking healthier, more convenient approaches to meal preparation.

Throughout this cookbook, we have explored a myriad of tantalising dishes ranging from traditional fish and chips and succulent roast dinners to scrumptious sweet delights. This diverse collection addresses every dietary preference and lifestyle: vegetarians, vegans, pescatarians and carnivores alike have all had their tastes satiated in extraordinary fashion.

Health-conscious gourmands have undoubtedly discovered numerous benefits from our recipe collection. The air fryer enables individuals to prepare delicious meals while significantly reducing fat content. It delivers perfectly cooked, delectable cuisine without compromising nutritional values, challenging preconceived notions of healthful eating as dull or bland.

Environmental concerns remain foremost in contemporary societies, and this cookbook also embraces sustainability principles. As demonstrated throughout the book, air fryers consume less energy compared to traditional cooking methods. By reducing energy consumption and lowering carbon footprints, we not only enjoy our beloved culinary creations but do so with greater ecological responsibility.

As you close this book's pages, may your air frying experiences flourish, allowing you to savour countless delightful meals shared with family and friends. May this cookbook endure as a cherished tome within your home library - a testament to culinary experimentation and progressive gastronomy that honours the indomitable spirit of British cuisine.

Printed in Great Britain
by Amazon

24660325R00051